Rabbiting

With Ferret, Dog, Hawk and Gun

Rabbiting

With Ferret, Dog, Hawk and Gun

Seán Frain

The Crowood Press

First published in 2005 by
The Crowood Press Ltd
Ramsbury, Marlborough
Wiltshire SN8 2HR

www.crowood.com

British Library Cataloguing-in-Publication Data
A catalogue record for this book is available from the British
Library.

ISBN 1 86126 802 5

Dedication
This book is dedicated to all true countrymen.

Acknowledgements
My sincerest thanks must go to the following people for their
assistance with this book: Shane Southern, Derek Webster, Chris
Dewhurst, Barry and Danny Hill, Carl Noon, as well as all those
fascinating characters with whom I hunted as a young lad. Also,
thanks to the *Countryman's Weekly* for their support.

Typeset by Servis Filmsetting Ltd, Manchester

Printed and bound in Great Britain by Cromwell Press, Trowbridge

CONTENTS

CHAPTER 1

THE YOUNG ENTRY

'T'best rabbitin' ferret int' north o' England!' I had been told when I went to purchase the huge hob that was bounding around all over the place, trying – in vain – to draw me into his little game. The rabbit warren appeared to be well used: the runs leading to and from it were a veritable motorway of 'coney' activity, and the vast amount of droppings all around were also a positive indication of plenty of rabbits; but even so, Ben – that big, fat polecat type with the generous layers of lard rippling as he jumped about me in typical ferret fashion – would not enter that lair and disappear below ground as he was supposed to.

I couldn't believe it. That huge, fat ferret had obviously been tried by his previous owner and found wanting, and I had proved to be the proverbial born sucker! Work, it seemed, just wasn't in him: he was such a happy fellow, and all he wanted to do was to play his daft games, bounding around all over the place and chattering noisily as he went. Every time I reached for him, he evidently thought I was joining in, and he would bound around even more, avoiding my hand so that I couldn't pick him up. And whenever I did succeed in grabbing him, he would twist and turn and squirm about, and as soon as I placed him on the ground again, directly in front of those enticing tunnels with the hot, tempting scent of bunny wafting out of the darkness, he simply went on with his silly game. I had every reason to be annoyed, I suppose, but I just couldn't get mad with him; in fact, he proved such a charming little chap that I even ended up laughing and playing along with him, despite my lack of success at becoming a seasoned rabbit hunter.

This was the pattern my first few rabbiting trips followed, and my frustration continued to build until, finally, I was on the verge of giving up. I had grown very attached to Ben, but he just wasn't earning his keep. He was also one of the largest ferrets I have ever come across and had quite an appetite, almost eating me (or rather, my mother) out of house and home. I thought it only fair that he caught some of his own food, but he didn't seem too willing a participant in this arrangement, and continued to do little else but play. That is when I decided to enlist the help of someone who had quite a few years' experience of hunting rabbits with ferrets.

Some Expert Advice

First of all I was told that Ben must get rid of his surplus weight. Then I was to teach him that dark tunnels could be places of great interest and rich reward: I had to construct an artificial tunnel system and place little treats inside, such as raw liver; once he had found these, he would learn to explore dark passages eagerly, and thus would soon become an effective bolter of rabbits lurking below ground. With much excitement, I immediately set about putting this plan into effect.

My tunnel system consisted of books piled on each side as walls, with more books balanced on the top of these as a roof, making a dark and inviting tunnel. I then placed small pieces of meat in different locations within the 'subterranean' system. After waiting a little while to allow the scent of the meat to drift through the dark passages, I then placed the slimmer, but still huge, Ben at the entrance and hoped for the best. Typically, he leaped into the air, twisted around and began bounding and chattering all over the place, bumping into the entrance of the tunnel system and causing it to collapse: a disastrous first effort! But I was determined to succeed, and so quickly rebuilt my fake rabbit warren and tried again.

As I placed him on the ground, he began cavorting around, making it difficult for me to keep a firm hold on him. But then, just as I loosed him, he suddenly stopped messing about and remained still, his nose wrinkling as though he had caught the scent of something that interested him: at long last he moved towards the darkness, and finally disappeared into the tunnel. The trouble was, his huge bulk filled the narrow passage and caused the tunnel to collapse in places, with books moving along and piling up as they rode on his back. Nevertheless, despite this technical problem, he managed to find his first quarry, a delicious (according to a ferret's taste, of course) piece of raw liver that he gulped down with much relish. He then moved on to investigate further, and was soon coming upon even more little treats. By this time the tunnel system was a complete shambles, but that didn't matter, for

Ben was now exploring with purpose, having quickly grasped the point of all this tunnel hunting.

I had been told always to make sure that he was hungry before using this method, and it began working very well indeed, though I had to make the system somewhat larger in order to prevent the 'tunnels' collapsing. Now and then he would still relapse, however, suddenly leaping into the air, his loud chattering echoing around the dark passages, and bumping into the books, frequently causing large parts of the artificial tunnel to subside. But no matter, he was now slimmer and keen to explore dark tunnels in search of goodies – in other words, he was ready to enter. And I felt that at last I, too, was ready to enter; because despite all my efforts – all the hours of wandering around the countryside in search of bunnies – I was yet to catch my first rabbit. The trouble was, at that time I really knew nothing about rabbits: I was just thirteen years of age, and I hadn't been able to find any book that told me about ferrets and ferreting, and simply tried my ferret at anything that looked like a hole. But with the breakthrough with Ben, at last I felt I was getting somewhere.

My First Proper Rabbiting Trip

Autumn had arrived and I had been asked to accompany a local man on a rabbiting trip into the hills. Declan Feeney, known simply as Dec to his friends, was somewhat of a rogue who spent much of his time poaching. He was out of ferrets at that time and had heard that I owned one, which was why he had asked me to accompany him on this, my first proper outing. I

Like Danny Hill (pictured with his two working polecat jills), I was a young lad when I began ferreting.

worried that if it turned out that Ben had learned nothing from my rigorous training programme, then this could be a most embarrassing day for me. I could see it only too clearly: Ben bounding around the well-used entrance full of scent and rabbit droppings, and keenly marked by Dec's lurcher; and me, red-faced, trying frantically to get him to go below ground, stuffing his huge frame into the entrance out of desperation – and as soon as I released my

hold, the massive, stupid ferret, mouth ajar and chattering wildly, rushing out at me, overjoyed that I was joining in his silly games.

I was flushed with embarrassment at the very thought of it, and almost backed out; but Dec was now tapping on the front door (it was first light and the rest of the family was still in bed), his lurcher by his side, keen to get started.

We headed off into the hills, the chill of

that autumn morning nipping at our ears, noses and fingers, the sounds of the blackbirds and the gulls high overhead, on their way to more traditional feeding grounds on the east coast no doubt, breaking the silence of the dawning day. The woods were still and calm in the windless morning, the russet and golden colours of the dying leaves contrasting starkly against the backdrop of the green hills. Ben was secure in his sack, sleeping again after he had been so rudely disturbed at such an unsociable hour; and Cassy, Dec's lurcher, walked with bounding steps beside us, trembling not with the cold, but with keen anticipation. This was my first proper rabbiting trip, and I was looking forward to it with great eagerness.

In the past I had spent quite some time shoving my ferret at holes, which I found everywhere, but I had yet to see a real live rabbit. Yet one of the first things that struck me that morning was the sheer abundance of them, and I wondered what I had been doing wrong. The fields held plenty, sitting out feeding in the dull light of early morning, and bobbing white tails everywhere. They had seen us coming and had scattered immediately, some heading into the warrens, while others sat nearby, watching to see what we would do in the safe knowledge that their sanctuary was just a few steps away.

At home, Ben was by this point in time entering and exploring my fake tunnel system without any hesitation whatsoever, and he had been amply rewarded for his efforts. But on this occasion there were no fake tunnel systems: this was the real thing and, come what may, this morning I was going to find out exactly what he was made of. Cassy remained by the side of her master, now held on a slip, a thin piece of leather placed round her neck:

simply release one side of this, and the dog was free to give chase. Dec ignored the runners because they were too far off and much too close to refuge, and waited his chance. We walked down through a small wood and entered the pasture where we had seen plenty of rabbits on the move – though usually there are always sitters, too, crouching in the grass and hoping to avoid detection.

Coursing with Cassy

Dec scanned the field and then began heading out into the open grasslands. I, too, had scanned the field, but could not tell a cowpat from a bunny and so made quite a few false alarms. Dec quickly dismissed these, his experienced eye instantly recognizing what was, and what was not, his intended quarry. Once a sitter was spotted, he made his way slowly towards it, and Cassy fixed her eyes intently on the spot, slowly descending into a crouch, ready for immediate action. Quite some ground can be made on a sitter as long as you avoid making any panic-stricken rush; but on this morning the sitters were soon up and running before the hunter and his dog had gained much ground on them, and so Cassy had quite a hard time. She was a fast little bitch, a whippet/greyhound cross, but the distances did not leave her with much of a chance, and one run after another ended with the rabbit disappearing into a warren and the little bitch standing there, bewildered, disappointed, looking into the darkness of the tunnel.

I was a little nervous, but was still keen to try Ben; but Dec had other ideas. He wanted to move on and course as many rabbits as possible while they were still out feeding, and then ferret some of the warrens later, on the way back. He said that this would also leave time for those bunnies to forget about the danger above ground, which would mean they would bolt more readily.

As the morning wore on, the wind began to blow and to steadily increase until the day was blustery indeed; leaves fell from the dense woodlands and were scattered across the fields, and the cloud shadows chased across the face of the hills at a rapid pace. Most of the rabbits had now gone from their feeding grounds and were sleeping the day away: it was time to give Ben a try at last. Cassy had enjoyed some fast bursts of speed in pursuit of coney, but had failed to catch, and I just hoped Ben could come up with the goods and provide us with a rabbit for her to catch.

Ben Enters at Last

We climbed the high wall and dropped into the sparse woodland above a small reservoir, used for fishing by the workforce of a nearby factory. These people would spend all week working long hours inside that factory, and would then spend the whole of their weekend sitting fishing in its shadow! I thought this was strange, especially as this area has several excellent fishing venues up in the hills, or in the middle of woodland and pasture, which to my mind were far more charming places to enjoy a day out. Anyway, this place held a good number of rabbits and Cassy was immediately in action, marking a small warren close to the stone wall we had just climbed over. She stood there, just staring into the hole, but very intently, with one of her front paws raised, and trembling violently. This, Dec assured me, was a sure sign that this warren was occupied.

Ah well, I thought, there goes a good excuse if Ben won't enter. Before that I could simply have laughed it off if he wouldn't go to ground, saying that there couldn't be anything at home – but not now. Dec had grown to trust his lurcher after many ferreting trips, and so would know if it was my ferret at fault, were things to go drastically wrong. A ferret refusing to work is not such a huge catastrophe, true, but to a thirteen-year-old boy who wishes to impress an experienced rabbit hunter, nothing, at that moment, could have been of more importance. I placed the sack on the ground and untied it, and Ben popped his huge head out (and once again, it made me feel sure there was a little grizzly bear somewhere in his make-up!).

I lifted him out and placed him on the mound of sand at the entrance, hoping that he would simply disappear below ground. However, even before I let go of him, I knew that things threatened to take a turn for the worst, because I could feel him twisting around as I gripped his massive bulk. Sure enough, as I let go, reluctantly, apprehensively, he began dancing around and chattering cheerfully, his mouth wide open as he charged at me, then suddenly turning, bounding away, scattering sand into my eyes in his wake. I reached for him, flushed with embarrassment, but he simply avoided me and bounded around even more wildly. He had been disturbed early on, but had made up for it since, sleeping soundly as I carried him in that sack and enjoying a wonderful lie-in; and this had greatly refreshed him and restored his good humour after such an early morning call, and it showed now as he worked off that excess energy with great enthusiasm. Dec didn't say anything, but I could sense his dour gaze upon me and my ferret, his impatience growing as the two fools messed about in front of that warren. I began to feel unbearably uncomfortable, especially as my efforts to get another hold on my ferret were badly failing. Just as things could not get any worse, Ben bounded away from me and bumped into the entrance of the warren with such force that I am sure the ground shook; certainly it was enough to alert those sleeping bunnies of 'danger' above ground. Sand fell from the worn sides of the hole, and some fell on Ben's big daft head. He shook himself vigorously, and I was waiting for his game to begin again – when he suddenly stopped dead in his tracks, sniffing the air, his nose wrinkling from side to side.

Unbelievably he began moving forwards, his demeanour now much more serious and intent, until at *last* he disappeared into the darkness of the warren. This was not a big place: in fact, it was an ideal burrow for starting a novice, just two or three holes and really quite shallow. A moment or two of silence then followed, broken only by the scuttling of blackbirds feeding among the debris below nearby bushes, the squabbling of a pair of mallard out on the water, the rustling of the dry, dead leaves and the occasional birdsong from the branches of the trees towering above us. And then there were loud thumping and bumping sounds from below, and it was obvious, even to a first-timer like me, that Ben was at last doing the job he was bred for.

The bumps grew ever nearer, ever

Ben at last entered!

louder, until, there, just inside the entrance, appeared the head of a large rabbit. It was obviously unable to move, and we could only assume that Ben had a firm hold of its back end. Ferrets are incredibly quick when they strike at their prey, and they can match a rabbit for speed over the first couple of feet or so. Ben had obviously done so with this one and had caught hold of it just before it got out into the open. The weight he had lost had no doubt helped his fast striking ability, and I congratulated myself for listening to the advice I had been given. Those methods had worked after all, and I had avoided major embarrassment. Ben was now a working ferret.

Dec reached into the hole and dragged out the rabbit with Ben attached, and quickly despatched it. Ben had released his hold – and suddenly that daft, playful look had gone from his face. He was now a much more serious ferret who had very quickly matured, now that he knew what life was all about.

It was now getting late in the day and we decided to make our way home across easier country. Those other rabbits could wait for another day. Dec held on to Ben's rabbit, and I waited for him to hand it over as we parted – but he didn't. I was only a young lad and much smaller than him, so I decided to say nothing as he walked away with my prize, for I was sure that discretion was the better part of cowardice! No matter: my ferret and I, both of us having qualified as 'young entry', had at last succeeded in what we were both born to do, and vital lessons had been learned, lessons that could only be built on as we gained more experience in the field.

CHAPTER 2

A HISTORY OF THE HUNTED RABBIT

Rabbits were introduced to British shores by the Normans at some time during the twelfth century, and for two vital reasons: as a supply of fresh, readily available meat; and for their good quality fur, which would help to keep families warm during the severe winter months. Rabbits have three layers of hair: a very dense, soft undercoat, through which longer hairs protrude that are much stronger, and give the rabbit a great deal of its colour; and a third layer where the hairs are even longer, but are far less abundant, rather scattered in amongst the others. So it is easy to understand why the French invaders valued this small animal so highly.

The Rabbit's Value

As a readily available source of fresh meat the rabbit was ideal because it was small, and this was particularly relevant during the summer months when meat could go off very quickly indeed, especially in hot or thundery weather; this could cause

Rabbits are a ready source of fresh meat and fur.

'stomach bugs', even life-threatening ones. Slaughtering any large meat animal, such as a bullock or a pig, in summer could be risky unless there was a community large enough to share in its consumption. Rabbits, being small, could be killed and finished in just one meal, two at the most; so not only was rabbit meat a very good source of necessary goodness such as vitamins and protein, it was also very practical and could be eaten fresh after the kill. And rabbits were quite easily attainable, too.

Coney beds were surrounded by pasture and, very often, large stone walls that were tightly built in order to prevent rabbits escaping. When they were needed as meat, they were ferreted: nets were placed over the holes, and dogs, or, much later, guns would be waiting to account for those that bolted. Nothing was wasted: the rabbit would be carefully skinned and the pelt dried out for use later on. The liver, kidneys and heart would have been eaten, and the head would no doubt have gone to feed either ferret or dog. Dogs would also eat the legs and part of the paws.

Once those pelts had been stitched together and garments made, the triple-layered fur would give a great deal of protection against the vicious elements. Remember, these were times long before global warming had caused the milder winters that we are used to, and the landscape was often snowbound for weeks on end. These days we have the inconvenience of snow for a day or two at the most. True, now and again we might have a fall of snow that covers the land for maybe a couple of weeks, if, and when, we have a more typical winter; but these conditions are still relatively insignificant when compared to winters in those days, when snow and ice were often still part of the scene well into springtime.

I was talking to Brian Nuttall about coat type in terriers, and how this seems far less important these days, given the much milder winters year after year. He can well remember those days when true winters held the land in a vice-like grip, when a good, dense 'jacket' was of great importance on a working dog. Nevertheless, it is his belief that sooner or later we are bound to get a severe winter, and that many of today's terriers will then suffer because their coats are so lacking in truly dense, warm fur.

He also observed that many farmers are now lambing much earlier, even in January in some cases, in order to have lambs ready to sell fat in late summer/early autumn; and he considered that they, too, might well be 'caught out' were we to have a more typical, colder winter, and could risk losing many to adverse weather conditions. And certainly if we were to have deep snow and hard frosts in the latter part of winter, as was the norm at one time, then lambs would perish if farmers were not able to house them, and had to leave them outside in harsh conditions. At one time, lambs were not seen until the latter half of March, when the weather was a little kinder (as compared to January and February temperatures). During those severe winters, which now seem a distant memory, there is no doubt that many families depended on the warmth of their clothes made from rabbit fur in order to survive.

Thus rabbit meat became readily available – and even during the hot summer months, as we have seen – it was extremely cheap to produce, and was very nutritious. In those days, as well as up until recent times, the rabbit played a very important part in the rural economy, and landowners would make quite a lot of money from 'harvesting' their coney beds

The warrener's dog would retrieve live to hand.

and selling them for both their meat and their fur. Virtually every part of the rabbit could be used as food or clothing, with only the ears, the pads and claws of the feet, as well as the intestines of course, left to go to waste – though no doubt a use was found even for these, in days gone by!

For hundreds of years this system was employed, and the humble rabbit played a very important part in the feeding and clothing of the British people. So these coney beds proved to be very useful indeed – but rabbits are athletic, determined individuals, and escapes were inevitable, especially from enclosures that were not maintained properly (a criminal neglect in view of the income that rabbit meat and fur earned a country estate, for relatively little effort on the part of the landowner). Once built, coney beds needed only a few occupants, and then all one had to do was to sit back and wait just a few months. Rabbits are incredibly prolific breeders and multiply at an amazing rate; thus they would quickly fill the warren and pas-

ture, so that harvesting them became a positive necessity.

Even if a harvest were particularly ruthless and large numbers were taken, stocks would quickly be replenished during the long breeding season to come. Furthermore, ferreted rabbits, whether they hit the nets or were taken by dogs, could easily be released if they proved unsuitable – that is, if they were too young, or not quite up to the average weight (a netted rabbit can easily be 'turned down' unharmed). The dogs used would be soft-mouthed – they would grip their prey as gently as they could – and would release their hold immediately the owner offered his hand. This was absolutely necessary, for meat would be bruised and unsellable if a dog were hard-mouthed, crushing its quarry to death and piercing the flesh. Even if rabbits were shot, rather than netted or coursed with dogs, those that proved too small could be left to run on by a discerning, experienced shot.

The Rabbit as a Major Agricultural Pest

Poorly maintained enclosures thus enabled the rabbit to escape into the open, where they began to cause much damage to crops and good, rich grazing pasture; by the eighteenth century it had switched from being an important part of the rural economy, bringing in quite considerable sums of money for landowners who sold their stock for fresh meat and fur, to being a major agricultural pest: the rabbit was therefore now hunted for other reasons. True, in small, easily manageable numbers, rabbits actually benefit the countryside in many ways: for instance, where land is not cultivated, rabbits will suppress the growth of shrubs such as bramble and hawthorn scrub by nibbling at the young shoots and preventing them from growing beyond this stage. Thus wild flowers can flourish in many of these areas, and they in turn attract insects, which benefit different bird species.

Rabbits also have a habit of scraping the ground and even making short diggings into the turf. This is said to be a purely territorial practice, carried out by the dominant rabbits in the colonies, but I suspect it is also done in play by growing youngsters who are simply exercising their digging instinct, in preparation for later life when they may dig burrows themselves. By scraping the grass away and digging a little into the soil, rabbits will uncover worms and grubs, and this, too, benefits bird populations. Robins, for instance, will soon spot a rabbit carrying out this practice, and will quickly alight on the spot, grabbing and gulping down any juicy grubs that have been exposed by the activities of the bunnies.

Where rabbits are found in large numbers, they can ruin good grazing land.

The Effects of Rabbit Damage

On the down side, when they are left to get out of hand, large numbers of rabbits can cause severe problems for the landowners who once made a fortune out of them, and in particular this digging activity can have disastrous consequences. When only found in reasonable numbers, these scrapings cause very little damage, but I have seen pasture so badly scraped and dug that it was difficult to pick one's way between grass and exposed soil – and obviously the bare soil offers no grazing whatsoever for sheep and cattle. Some farms are so badly invaded by rabbits that what was once excellent grazing pasture is now completely ruined and can only support a few beasts, rather than a herd or a flock of any number.

Furthermore, because rabbits are such prolific breeders, they are rarely found in reasonably low numbers, except perhaps where they have been decimated by disease. When pasture is so badly affected a farmer may be forced to rent better grazing land elsewhere, and this can then completely undermine his profit margins and therefore seriously affect his livelihood.

Rabbit Hierarchy and Lifestyle

The rabbit colony has dominant members who can be either male or female, and these rule the warren system; generally they will not tolerate subordinates within their territory. The more dominant members are also the most likely to breed.

Rabbits graze mostly at dawn and dusk, and a 'sentry' will be put on guard whilst they do so: a mound of earth full of rabbit droppings can be safely assumed to be the local 'watchtower'. Rabbits crop the grass and other vegetation so short there is precious little left that would provide safe cover, and the majority therefore relies on the sentry to alert them to any danger. From such an elevated place as our mound the open area is easily watched over by the sentry on duty; and in the event of any perceived danger it will thump the ground with its powerful hind legs. In fact, in many areas countrymen refer to rabbits as 'thumpers' or 'drummers' because of this warning signal, which is very effective indeed, for a 'drumming' rabbit can easily be heard at quite some distance. Also, the bobbing white underside of the sentry's tail as it heads for the safety of the warren serves as a warning for all the others to be on full alert.

When danger does threaten, as it often does, then some will go straight inside the relative safety of their underground lairs, while others will simply move closer to the warren and wait and see if danger comes any nearer. A small percentage will simply

Feeding rabbits always have a lookout posted, which makes stalking them challenging, whether it is with gun, hawk or lurcher.

squat where they are feeding: these are known as 'sitters' and are the most likely to fall victim to predators.

The 'Sitter'

Lurchers waiting for a bolt.

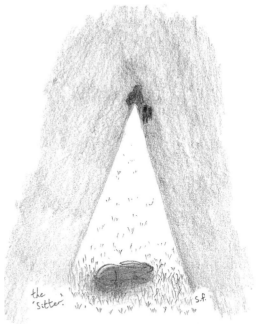

The 'sitter'.

A 'sitter' can often escape danger because it is not easily seen: for instance, if a fox or a stoat, or some other predator, misses the drifting scent of a squatting rabbit, then that rabbit is likely to escape. Those who hunt rabbits at night with the use of a lamp will be very familiar with 'sitters', for very often, as the beam sweeps the field, a good number of them, especially if they have not been lamped before, will squat immediately. If a lurcher does not quickly learn to watch out for these, many will escape, for the dog will overrun the quarry and then, if the rabbit bolts, it can very often make it to safety long before the dog has had time to turn and recover.

On one occasion I spent a few days hunting rabbits on North and South Uist in the outer Hebrides, staying with Tim Green and Sue Rothwell of The Plummer Terrier Club of Great Britain, and we came across a 'sitter' that would have done better had it headed for its warren. We were hunting the flatlands by the sea on South Uist: rabbits are found in large numbers here because they live and feed amongst the rich marram grasses of this area. We pulled up by a large warren surrounded by several feeding rabbits; as we climbed out of the vehicle, many of them disappeared below ground, while a few others just moved in a little closer and watched us. As we walked towards them, however, these simply hopped away a few paces and were also quickly inside.

Tim, however, had seen just one of the rabbits squat immediately we got out of

Waiting, waiting! Merab, from Plummer's old strain.

the vehicle, and called his lurcher, Merab, a descendant of Brian Plummer's old strain of running dog, over to him and headed for the spot. The rabbit was impossible to see amongst the vegetation, but Tim knew he was in the right area. Suddenly it exploded from the ground and headed towards the warren: but Merab sprang into action and quickly gained on her quarry, catching it just before it reached safety, her head almost disappearing inside the sandy entrance of the burrow.

Some 'sitters' have even been caught by the hunter simply walking over and picking them up, or knocking them on the head with a stick. I have also known a hunter nudge one with his boot in order to get it running, such is the determination of some rabbits to squat rather than make a run for it. Usually though, as danger gets ever nearer, a rabbit will suddenly spring into action and make for the nearest warren.

Norman Mursell in his book *Come Dawn, Come Dusk* mentions an occasion when quite a large number of rabbits were so terrified by the rising floodwaters of a local river that they were easily taken by just hitting them with a stick. Sometimes when rabbits are terrified they appear to be shocked into immobility, and these are easily taken by predators, including man. This is occasionally seen in a rabbit that is being hunted by a stoat, when for some reason it will 'freeze', and is then easily caught: one can only assume this reaction is caused by terror. The hunter of rabbits often benefits from this action of 'sitting', or squatting, when danger threatens.

Rapid Reproduction

Once it had escaped captivity, the rabbit began to breed in the wild, and its numbers swelled at an incredible rate. Rabbits are sexually mature at an early age, around sixteen weeks old, and can have several litters in one year; in fact as one litter leaves the care of its mother, another quickly replaces it. The young are born in a separate tunnel known as a 'stab', or a 'stop', and this is necessary because buck rabbits will often kill young babies, if given the chance to do so. This 'nursery' can be found within the main burrow system, but very often it is dug well away from there, and when the doe is not feeding or cleaning the young, the entrance is filled in temporarily to prevent the risk of predators, and buck rabbits of course, finding and killing them. Even so, many are found, dug out and killed – but another litter will quickly replace those lost, and

these will, in turn, be ready for breeding in just a few weeks after leaving the 'stop': so it is easy to understand how rabbit numbers can multiply so rapidly, despite the fact that the rabbit has so many enemies.

Man in Pursuit of the Rabbit

Man pursues the rabbit mercilessly. He uses dogs and ferrets, the lamp at night, long nets, purse nets, snares, guns, and even a system of blocking the entrance to the rabbit's tunnel so that it is stopped just inside; he does this during their nightly feeding times, then disturbs them so they run back to their warren, but can only get down into their hole for a short distance. The hunter then simply puts his hand in and pulls out the helpless victim. Easy – too easy, in fact – though this method does

Ferrets have been used by man for centuries.

Dogs would be used to take rabbits bolted from coney beds.

carry risks. In his interesting book *Rogues and Running Dogs*, Brian Plummer mentions a poaching expedition where this method of taking large hauls of rabbits was used, but in the course of which he was badly bitten by a *rat* that had sought refuge in the blocked tunnel meant for a rabbit. Stoats, even mink or polecats, could also be lurking in that passage when a poacher reaches in for his rabbit, and one can easily imagine the damage that could be done in such a situation. This method of catching rabbits is not often used, however, because the work involved in blocking off those tunnels is very intensive, and there are better (not to mention safer) methods that can be employed instead.

Foxes feed mainly on rabbits, as do birds of prey such as buzzards. These are carrion eaters, true, but buzzards will also take live rabbits, especially when they have young to feed. Stoats, weasels, badgers, otters, mink, wild and feral cats, even domestic cats in some areas, will all take and feed on rabbits, and one begins to wonder how on earth they survive, let alone thrive, with so many odds stacked against their survival. Yet not only *do* rabbits survive, but they continue to be a major agricultural pest in most areas, despite the fact that, since the early 1950s, they have been decimated by a far deadlier enemy than either man or beast.

The Deadly Effects of Myxomatosis

Man is capable of incredible cruelty, both towards animals as well as to his own kind, and nothing has so far surpassed this capability with more savage effect than the introduction of a flea-borne disease known as myxomatosis in 1954. Rabbits suffer terribly when afflicted with this disease, and initially wiped out up to 95 per cent of the rabbit population. Not only did this have a devastating effect upon the rural economy, since rabbit meat quickly became considered inedible by the general public, but it also meant starvation and death for scores, even hundreds, of foxes, buzzards, stoats and other animals that depended on the once large population of this readily available food source; the fox population declined dramatically after the destruction wrought by this terrible plague. The introduction of myxomatosis – a decision made, it must be said, with the full backing of the government at the time – did, however, achieve its objective: that of reducing damage to pasture and crops.

Thankfully the rabbit is a very hardy creature and it quickly began to build up a certain resistance: by the 1970s it was once again proving to be a major pest in many areas – though at not quite the same level of intensity as before the disease was introduced. Poachers in particular were hit hard after myxomatosis had caused carnage in the countryside, for the market collapsed literally overnight. And because many of the buying public had witnessed for themselves the terrible sight of huge numbers of rabbits blindly and weakly stumbling around a field, or simply sitting there waiting to die, as a result many were immediately put off this once highly valued meat source, and so game dealers and butchers no longer bought them. Poachers therefore turned to more profitable avenues of making a living, such as the taking of deer and pheasants, rather than starving, or finding themselves a more legitimate form of employment.

The Rabbit Poacher

Up until myxomatosis, rabbits were poached in huge numbers, and very often this activity was tolerated by keepers up and down the country, for rabbits were pests and gamekeepers were often far too busy to devote much time to attempting to reduce the population on their estates. Control, however, was essential, for each country estate would have several farms on its land, and these were threatened by a large population of coney. Crops were severely damaged and good pasture ruined, for rabbits scrape the ground, and their urine and droppings can kill off all but the hardiest of plants.

Also, rabbits often dig burrows out in the middle of pastureland, and cattle and horses have been known to fall into these holes and break a leg, so it was essential that gamekeepers made time for catching as many rabbits as possible. Along with organized shoots, when local farmers were invited to take part, keepers would snare and shoot rabbits as often as they could; but as already stated, only a limited amount of time could be devoted to such 'less important' activities. Hence the reason for many being not too hard on rabbit poachers.

These poaching gangs were often from nearby towns, or even cities, though some were local farm workers who supplemented their living – usually on or below the breadline – with a few rabbits taken each week. Some of these would undoubtedly be sold to the less choosy game dealers, or even restaurants and public houses that put on food; most, however, would help feed their own families and any animals they kept, such as dogs. Making a living was far from easy for many of these workers, and before the days of myxomatosis the rabbit did much to reduce the hardships that poverty brings.

Large hauls can be taken using ferrets and dogs.

The Poacher and the Gamekeeper

This tolerance by keepers often led to a somewhat blasé kind of attitude in some poachers, and one of these was James Hawker. In his published journal *A Victorian Poacher* (an interesting, but very badly written book – although it was never intended for publication), he records how he would use a shotgun, even during daylight hours, for his poaching activities, though he would take far more than just rabbits from a country estate.

True, gamekeepers would still make an effort to catch poachers, often waiting near to where a snare had been discovered, knowing full well that a poacher would soon come along in order to check if he had been successful; or waiting where a pile of nets had been left in the undergrowth, or where bicycles had been discovered, left behind a wall or some other out-of-the-way place. But even then, after catching them – sometimes in the very act of ferreting or long netting – they would simply give them a 'slap on the wrist' and send them packing with a few stern words. Norman Mursell tells of a number of these occasions when he was involved in apprehending poachers on the Eaton estate and of how they were dealt with. Of course, it depended on what type of game was being poached, but rabbit hunters were often let off very lightly indeed, though without their catch, of course. In fact, the keepers at Eaton had a very effective way of dealing with poachers: they took their names and addresses, and made them pay money to local charities, such as the hospital fund, rather than making a fuss and involving the law.

Other gamekeepers were not so tolerant, however, and were always involving the police, even for rabbits; or they sometimes dispensed their own 'justice', often leaving the victims in dire need of medical assistance. The keepers knew that no complaints would be taken to the police, for their victims had been poaching in the first place and were not in any position to be reporting anything illegal that had been done to them. But in these instances, the poachers, many of whom were originally only after rabbits, would get their revenge by moving on to the estate's pheasant, partridge and deer: so in the long run, a severe beating for the poacher usually had adverse repercussions for the keepers, and it was far better for them to deal fairly with the miscreants and punish them according to the quarry being poached. Of course, when pheasant and deer were being taken, the keepers had no choice but to involve the law; but many would not be too hard on those who supplemented an often meagre living by selling and putting on the table a few rabbits.

Poaching Methods

Poachers in those days had many crafty ways of taking rabbits, and still use these ways today, though more in the interests of controlling rabbits for troubled farmers, than for poaching their own; for the rabbit has failed to realize a decent price since those catastrophic days of myxomatosis, and so is not really a viable option for those who wish to make a living this way. Some do continue to supplement their livelihood by putting rabbit meat on the table, and by selling a few to game dealers with a faithful clientèle who still appreciate this source of good fresh meat.

Snares can be a very effective way of taking rabbits, but they must be set properly so that foxes, badgers, cats and dogs do not get caught in them. They are placed along much used rabbit runs, and can be a useful way of poaching bunnies from private land, because a poacher can set a snare and be away very quickly indeed. The only trouble with snaring is that, if a snare is discovered by a keeper, all he has to do is to wait in the undergrowth for the poacher to return, intent on checking if he has been successful or not, and catch him red-handed. Many poachers have been caught out in this way, very often in the act of removing a rabbit from the snare itself, something which would surely guarantee a successful conviction if the keeper wished to involve the law, though this was rarely the case.

Poaching continues today, but there are far fewer country estates with resident gamekeepers nowadays, and so the impact of poaching is felt far less, even though rabbits and other game are still taken. Farmers regard rabbits as pests anyway, and so while they are perhaps not too happy about people tramping across their land without permission, they will probably not miss the rabbits taken – even the poaching of deer and pheasant would possibly not cause a farmer too much concern. Few know they have deer on the land in the first place, and they don't worry about the taking of pheasants since small shoots often rent the shooting rights and release a small number of pheasant for a few days of rough shooting. It is these who suffer when poachers take pheasant. Many of these shooting syndicates are made up of working-class men, so poachers these days can hardly claim to be taking from those who can afford the loss anyway!

Some poachers, like James Hawker mentioned earlier, rather than silently crossing a country and taking rabbits with snares, or by some other relatively unintrusive means, would be bold enough actually to ferret a country estate and shoot the bolting rabbits. This was an incredibly brazen thing to do, and one that could be easily apprehended; nevertheless, it was a much used method by some, and they usually got away with it. On more than one occasion, Hawker hid his gun as a keeper or a farmer approached, and was asked if he had seen anyone shooting on their land!

Declan Feeney, Brazen Poacher

Declan Feeney was one of the most brazen poachers I have ever known, and on more than one occasion he was known to have helped himself, not only to the game on a farmer's land, but also to the farmer's livestock and goods. Whilst out lamping, he would sometimes pay a visit to the farm itself and 'remove' some goods for himself: for instance, on one night he stole almost a score of fattened chickens from a farm, and these were used to feed his family and his dogs for quite a few weeks afterwards. He was quite fearless, despite the fact that he was thin and lightly built, and took many risks whilst involved in his illegal way of life, rarely, if ever, worrying about getting caught. This particular incident did backfire on him, however, for he quickly discovered that he had 'lifted' a bunch of old broilers which, when cooked, were exceedingly tough; his family gave up trying to enjoy them, and even the dogs only ate them reluctantly!

On another occasion, after a hard night's lamping, Dec and his poaching gang stopped off at a farm on the way home, as they fancied 'picking something up' for breakfast when they reached home. Dec then stealthily and silently crept over and around six sleeping Dobermanns in

order to steal a box containing seventeen dozen eggs! Those lamping nights were long and hard – and I should know, because I had begun accompanying Dec and, on occasion, his gang, on those nightly forays; rabbits were hunted in the main, with occasionally a hare added to the quarry list, but at least a good breakfast awaited our return: boiled eggs, poached eggs (literally!), fried eggs and scrambled eggs were all sampled during those early morning breakfasts, until the illegal supply ran out and it was back to plain old cereal. Dec loved his breakfast.

Rabbit meat became saleable again a few years after myxi had struck – although it has never reached the same popularity and value as in pre-myxi days – and Dec sold his rabbits to a game dealer who had a shop right in the heart of town; when passing, I often saw these hanging up in the window. His lurcher, Cassy, was a greyhound/whippet cross and she was a very useful lamping and daytime coursing bitch, often taking hares, especially when Dec travelled to Lincolnshire in order to course on the big flat fields of this area. His game dealer would take any hares he brought home, and so the venture was often a profitable one.

Dec only hunted rabbits by means of lurchers and ferrets, lamping, daytime coursing and ferreting being the methods he employed; but other poachers have used much more effective methods that have accounted for large numbers of coney. Dec could only sell on a few rabbits each week so there was no point in catching large hauls, but some dealers would take as many as they could get, especially during pre-myxomatosis days. When hunting rabbits in order to take large numbers, either for sale to a game dealer or simply for reasons of pest control, the long net would be used: this is a very efficient method, and one used widely by poachers and pest controllers alike.

Long Netting

Long netting is best carried out by two people, one to run out the net, while the other drives the pegs into the ground as silently as possible, at intervals of five or six yards. This method can be carried out by just one man, but it then takes much longer, and retrieving the haul afterwards would be a difficult task for a lone poacher. The pair would work silently and quickly, and then the feeding rabbits would be disturbed so that they would begin to make their way, usually hurriedly, back to their warrens. The long net would have been carefully placed between the feeding grounds and the warrens, and so the bunnies soon became enmeshed in the trap. The poachers would then simply untangle them – in itself a task that can be complicated, but is perfected with experience – and put them in the game bag. Huge hauls could be taken in just one night, and a decent living was made by many poachers who used this method regularly.

There are hidden dangers, however, in using this method for catching rabbits. In his book *Rogues and Running Dogs* Brian Plummer mentions a rogue he once knew called Billy Robbins, and tells of how, whilst gate netting for hares one night, a fox was caught in the trap and bit the poacher several times before he realized it wasn't a hare that he had captured. The same difficulty can easily confront the long netter, for this method is carried out on pitch-black nights when it is impossible

Nets were used to catch many rabbits from coney beds.

to see exactly what has been enmeshed in the net, and more than one poacher has been injured by a fox, or some other hard-biting predator, that has been caught in the trap meant for rabbits.

The Continuing Threat of Myxomatosis

Despite the war waged against them, rabbits have survived, and in many areas they are thriving once more – though every few years a mutant form of myxomatosis strikes again and reduces the numbers considerably. Where they are found in larger numbers, however, a fresh outbreak of this terrible disease hardly seems to 'dent' the population. I have been hunting in some areas of the Yorkshire Dales where rabbits almost equal the numbers of pre-myxomatosis times in some places. Whenever this scourge hits again, which is usually every three to five years, many rabbits die, of course, but that hardly seems to make any impression. These areas are heavily hunted too, and a great deal of poaching also occurs, yet rabbits are everywhere; I have even found large warrens right by the side of country lanes up in the Dales, so much are they having to compete for territory.

At the other end of the scale, myxomatosis has struck and almost wiped out the rabbit population in some places. This happened in most parts of my hunt country a few years ago, and in places I thought they had died off completely, for there were no signs of rabbits anywhere. Even the dogs failed to find any – yet many of those areas are now recovered, and a healthy population can be found once more. I have a theory, which I shall explain directly, as to why an area seems devoid of

Terrier 'Mist' Enters to Rabbit

My terrier bitch, 'Mist', first entered to rabbit up in the Yorkshire Dales, and it was due to myxi that she had her first confidence-boosting ferreting trip. Not only did she mark warrens accurately from day one, the nets quickly filling up with bunnies that were bolted by a very good working albino jill, but she also caught her first rabbit above ground. There are massive areas covered by reedbeds in some areas of the Dales, and Mist was in her element, hunting that hot scent and putting up several rabbits that she chased keenly until they were lost in the undergrowth, or got to ground. One rabbit, however, wasn't quick enough, and she caught it after just a few feet of a lightning-quick run. The rabbit had myxi, and simply lacked enough speed to get away. It wasn't badly infected at all and may, in fact, have been in the latter stages of recovery; but still, it was not in prime condition and paid the ultimate price. With enemies abounding, rabbits need to be in top condition if they are going to survive for long.

rabbits, yet has a good recovery of numbers a short time later.

Of course, the rate at which coney breeds is a very important factor in this rapid recovery rate, but it does not explain why rabbits cannot be found in an area prior to this. When only a few rabbits are left after a severe outbreak of a deadly disease such as myxomatosis, which threatens to wipe them out completely, I believe that something is triggered in the metabolism and instinct of rabbits which affects both how they live and the scent they give off. Just as a vixen fox gives off little scent when pregnant and nursing young cubs, so do rabbits that are threatened with extinction from an area. I believe they become far more careful and spend most of their time either below ground, or in the heart of dense coverts where they are difficult to reach, giving off hardly any scent so that predators cannot detect them, thus making it impossible for a dog to mark a burrow, and especially a deep one. Scrapings are almost non-existent and droppings rarely found.

So does the instinct of rabbits, or any species threatened severely, tell them to keep a very low profile until numbers have recovered sufficiently to 'absorb' losses through predation? I firmly believe so, because I have found this in many areas. After myxi has broken out, rabbits have apparently completely disappeared from some areas, sometimes for a few years; yet all of a sudden the dogs begin finding them again, hiding in undergrowth and marking warrens that previously showed no signs of occupation.

Some may conclude that rabbits have simply spilled over from other areas round about, but that has not been the case, for I have found this happening in places that are surrounded by urban areas, or places where there are too few rabbits surrounding a particular location for over-spill to be a possibility. The only explanation is the theory I have put forward. I do not hunt rabbits during the spring and summer months, and sometimes when I have returned to an area in the autumn, rabbits have been found where last winter there seemingly were none. Rabbits breed from late January through to the end of July, so it is easy to see how numbers can quickly recover, even if there are only a few breeding pairs left in an area. During milder winters, however, rabbits often breed from early January through to the end of September, or even later in some cases.

When myxi mutates and strikes in an area where there has already been an outbreak, there is a measure of immunity and the effect is not so disastrous, and recovery is quite rapid. Many rabbits will quickly build up this immunity and large numbers will either survive, or not become infected in the first place. However, when myxi is taken from one area and artificially introduced into another, then the consequences can be dire. In my area of Lancashire we had no problems whatsoever with myxomatosis for many years – well over a decade, in fact – then suddenly we had a severe outbreak and the rabbits were hit so hard that, in many places, the population was seemingly wiped out, as already described. I wondered why. In other areas of the country, such as the Yorkshire Dales, the rabbit population certainly suffered, but not to the extent that I saw in Lancashire. In fact it was every bit as severe as the first introduction, and as much as 95 per cent of the population succombed to this dreadful disease. It wasn't until a few years later, when the population was fast recovering at last, that I found out why the outbreak had been so severe.

The Truth Revealed

My terriers had just flushed a few rabbits from a dense patch of undergrowth, and had chased them up the hill and then down into yet more undergrowth. A chap stood nearby, watching the antics of my terrier pack with great delight. He approached me afterwards and began reminiscing about days long past when he had enjoyed rabbiting with dogs and ferrets. Later in the conversation, he said that some of the areas he and his friend hunted had become a little depleted with bunnies, due mainly to the building boom of that time, not to mention more roads cutting through once totally rural and unspoilt places; and so they had decided to bring in quite a number of rabbits which would then help to boost the flagging population.

I knew immediately what he was going to say next: this was, that he and his hunting partner had taken a few trips to the Dales, had ferreted and netted several rabbits, and brought them back to Lancashire for release into the wild. And so they thought they had solved the problem of the ailing rabbit population. But I knew then why myxomatosis had broken out those few years ago, and why it had hit the population of this area so badly, and so effectively. Those Yorkshire rabbits had built up a measure of immunity to each mutation of this disease as it went through the different cycles. But our Lancashire bunnies had not been struck down with any form of myxi for several years, but were then subjected to a mutation that had naturally occurred in the native population of Yorkshire: this was why the North Riding bunnies had quickly become immune to the mutation, and why a great deal of those rabbits had either escaped infection, or had rapidly recovered from it. But not so our Lancashire bunnies: they were hit hard, their immune system being totally unprepared for this onslaught, which wreaked havoc among them. Even now, after a decade has passed, rabbits are still struggling to recover from that outbreak. There have been other outbreaks since, but thankfully, these did not hit so hard, due, obviously, to the natural build-up of immunity.

A good lesson I have learned from this episode: if an area becomes depleted of rabbits for whatever reason, *leave them to recover in their own good time.* Stop hunting those areas for a season or two, or for however long it takes, and go instead to places where they are still found in healthy numbers. Whatever you do, *do not be tempted* to take rabbits from other areas and introduce them to places where the number of coney has been hit severely, because far more harm could be caused by doing this, as in the decimating outbreak of myxi described above. It has been a few years now since the last outbreak of myxomatosis in this part of Lancashire, so maybe we have seen the worst. I hope so. Although rabbits are a nuisance in large numbers, they are now such an integral part of the British landscape that it is sad to see their numbers reduced to such an all-time low that one hardly ever sees them! Rabbits can also be affected by the VHD virus.

As I have said, myxomatosis strikes every few years in many areas, and if one is poaching and selling the meat, the market can quickly dry up in this situation, forcing the poacher to go further afield for his 'goods'. This disease does not affect humans, or the dogs and ferrets that are fed on myxied carcasses – but still, the sight of a diseased rabbit quickly puts one off eating such meat. I never eat myxied rabbits, but feed them to ferrets and dogs, though I remove the head and all the 'innards' before doing so. I normally give the heads to my ferrets, but the thought of them eating those pus-filled eyes does not appeal somehow, though polecats and stoats, not to mention foxes, badgers and other predators, will do so out in the wild. In fact, where there is an outbreak of myxomatosis, every fox in the neighbourhood will descend on the place in search of easily caught food. Buzzards too, will benefit from an outbreak of myxi, for they are lazy hunters, except, possibly, at nesting time and during a severe winter when hunger will drive them to greater effort.

A Day's Hunting with my Pack

Fresh outbreaks of myxomatosis seem to occur suddenly. After the summer 'off' season, in late August I went to check out one of the farms where I have permission to hunt, in readiness for a rabbiting trip that would begin the new season. I was there early, not long after dawn, and the fields were full of rabbits, their scrapings everywhere, ruining the good pasture where sheep and horses normally graze. I decided to make an early start, and set

about reducing the population to more reasonable proportions.

Along with John Hill, I was hunting a mixed pack of terriers and teckels (a type of dachshund) at the time, and these set about the horde of rabbits with gusto. Using a small pack of dogs is a very effective way of reducing a high rabbit population, for when they are found in large numbers, they are easier to catch for some reason. Once they have been thinned out, they then become much harder to catch, being more alert and quick to make a run for it. I do not know why it is, but 'sitters' are far more common where larger numbers of rabbits are found, and it is these that usually fall prey to the dogs.

The pack entered a large bramble

A rabbiting pack: a mixture of teckels (owned by John Hill) and terriers (owned by the author).

Jack Webster, Danny Dewhurst and Kim, with several rabbits taken.

thicket and a rabbit was quickly found. This one, however, was not a 'sitter', preferring to make a run for it. Fell came out of the undergrowth and pursued his rabbit across a few feet of open pasture, catching it quickly. There were no obvious signs of any disease, but something was worrying. That rabbit had seemed just a little on the dopey side: it had failed to get into top gear and had died as a result. Once out into the open, a rabbit will quickly flee from a terrier, but something had seemed lacking with this one's efforts. I wasn't too worried though and carried on regardless, hoping to shift a few more for the farmer during that first visit.

We crossed the large pasture, heading now for the hillside full of gorse bushes where rabbits abounded. They emerged at dusk and spent the night and early morning feeding among the surrounding fields which led up to the wind-scorched moorland high above. The heather was still in bloom and seemed to breathe a purple haze during warmer, sunnier days. Rabbits are thinner on the ground among these high places and are much harder to catch, being wilder and far more alert. They need to be, for there is far less cover on the moors and so they must be on their guard at all times, not only looking out for man with his ferrets and dogs, his hawk and gun, but also keeping out of the way of stoats, buzzards and the hardy hill foxes of this area. These moorland rabbits are quick-witted indeed and are a challenge for any lurcher, no matter how fleet of foot.

This day was drizzly and miserable and a heavy blanket of dark cloud had descended and obliterated the bleak landscape above, yet we pressed on, determined to make inroads into the vast numbers of rabbits inhabiting this area. A few strong, healthy rabbits eluded the pack easily, some going to ground, while others simply disappeared among the undergrowth; but another rabbit was soon caught after Mist shot underneath a small growth of gorse, catching her prey before it had a chance of even thinking of running. Sadly, the puffed-up eyes and the lack-lustre coat told an all-too-familiar tale. Myxi had reared its ugly head again and our efforts were now concentrated on putting the sufferers out of their misery.

The saddest part of the day was when Fell caught, or rather, picked up, a pathetic creature that I hardly recognized to be a rabbit, as it sat by a wall waiting to die. The scrawny frame and the unseeing eyes hardly moved as Fell ended its suffering with a crushing bite. With a heavy heart, we trudged back to the car, with only the first rabbit we caught fit to take home for ferret and dog meat, and I cursed, all the way, those incredibly cruel people who had introduced this awful disease into the long-suffering rabbit population. I found no signs of disease in that first rabbit, but still, I did not fancy eating it, so I skinned it and cooked it for the terriers. That bunny was such a good specimen that it fed the dogs for almost a week.

I have a great deal of respect for rabbits and hate to see a population decimated by myxomatosis; they are such an integral part of the countryside that it is sad to see their numbers so reduced in some places that they are no longer to be seen around at all. Nevertheless, the rabbit is an incredibly hardy creature, and continues to recover. In fact, the place I have just described has now recovered, and a healthy population is once again beginning to become a problem in this area. You just can't keep a good rabbit down!

CHAPTER 3

GOOD RABBITING GROUNDS

Rabbits can be found almost anywhere, so locating good rabbiting grounds is easy enough, though actually obtaining permission is not always so easy. In the days when rabbits were 'farmed' for their meat and fur, coney beds consisted of mounds of earth inside an enclosure. Of course, other warrens would be dug inside these enclosures, but rabbits were not content with these, and soon began to escape. From here, they would take up residence in any suitable location within easy striking distance of good pasture or plentiful crops. Once out of the enclosed coney beds, rabbits – being prolific breeders and becoming sexually mature at a very early age – soon

spread throughout the country; nowadays, in spite of the introduction of myxomatosis during the early 1950s, they can be found in any area where there is a sufficient supply of green grass or crops, from large fields to small allotments.

In more recent years the rabbit's ability to colonize an area, even a country, in a relatively short time was demonstrated yet again after their introduction to Australia. Just a few pairs of rabbits were released in New South Wales, yet it took only a few years for their offspring to multiply to millions and become a major nuisance. Rabbits compete with sheep for good grazing land, and have proved to be a serious

Dales country; excellent rabbiting grounds.

problem for sheep farmers both here and down under: all kinds of different methods of control have been used, from rabbit fencing, to shooting, to introducing myxomatosis, and a whole host of other different ways of killing this pest to agriculture, including ferrets – these are also used extensively in Australia, although the hardy rabbit continues to be gravely troublesome in that country.

Woodland, pasture, canal banks, river banks, railway embankments, motorway embankments, refuse tips, quarries, factory grounds, golf courses, parks, farm yards, even pine woods and forests, especially around the edges and clearings where grass will grow: all these locations are places where rabbits, very often in large numbers, are likely to be found. Of course, many of these places will be impossible to hunt, legally anyway, because it is so difficult to obtain permission. For instance, due mainly to more recent legislation regarding public health and safety – and, of course, an 'I will sue you' society – it is no longer possible to ferret railway embankments. These are great places for hunting rabbits, but are now out of bounds to those who respect the law and try to live by it.

Rabbiting along Unused Railway Lines

Fortunately there are still many miles of unused railway, and permission may be granted to hunt these. When I was a lad (and not too choosy about where I hunted, legally or otherwise) I hunted rabbits on a number of unused railways, and the harvest was rich indeed. I can remember several outings with Dec and other poachers as we ferreted and coursed rabbits in

these places. Bramble thickets abound along railway embankments, and a good bushing terrier will have several on the run from such places. We would stand in an adjoining field with our lurchers on the slip, while a brace of terriers worked through these thickets. A yapping terrier would signal a find, and before long a rabbit would suddenly explode from the undergrowth and make a run for it across the pasture. The lurchers caught many in this way, though several did escape, especially when the fields were small and the warrens nearby.

Bramble thickets are always fruitful hunting grounds, and many will be full of coney, even during broad daylight, rather than the early morning or evening when one would expect rabbits to be above ground. It may be the case that many of these rabbits actually live and breed above ground, shunning the musty chambers of the nearby warrens in favour of the fresh air and outdoor life. Certainly, after the introduction of myxomatosis in 1954, reports came in of rabbit nests being found above ground, both in this country and in Australia, and it is thought that this tendency had something to do with the survival rate of many of the rabbit populations, because non-burrowing rabbits are less prone to catching the disease. Either these rabbits *choose* to live and breed above ground, or they are females ousted from warrens by more dominant doe rabbits – although contradicting the 'evicted' theory is the fact that it is usually the more dominant females that actually mate successfully and rear youngsters.

It is my belief that, if this tendency began whilst myxomatosis was at its worst, as it is thought, then it was because many rabbits opted to live and breed above ground simply because the warrens

Chris Dewhurst with rabbits caught in typically good rabbiting country.

were full of stinking, rotting carcases. This tendency then persisted in a percentage of the species and may still be found today, especially among those bunnies that choose to spend the day in dense under-growth, rather than below ground.

It is certainly worth enquiring whether permission can be granted to work unused railway embankments, and your request may well be successful unless there are plans for the re-establishment of a work-ing railway – when your chances will be virtually nil. The two main railways that I used to hunt many years ago fell into disuse, but are now being used again, mainly by steam locomotives; and so a rich source of huntable rabbits has been lost for ever.

These embankments continue to hold a thriving population, and the pastures adjoining them do suffer considerable damage. Of course, one can lamp these pastures and course them during the early morning, for a farmer will be more than happy to grant his permission when damage is being done to his grazing land; but the most effective method would prob-ably be to snare the field side of the runs that lead on to the embankment. I person-ally do not like snaring and do not practise this method of catching rabbits, though I am well aware that in some areas it is the only viable option for the control of their numbers.

For instance, snaring is one of the meth-ods that has been extensively used by

Rabbits, Rats and Leptospirosis

Rabbits can be found in good numbers on refuse tips, but gaining permission to hunt them is very often impossible. I hunted a tip near Bolton in Lancashire that was overrun with rabbits. They lived quite happily alongside rats (though rats will kill and eat baby rabbits, if they can find them young enough) and on several occasions I have bolted rats and rabbits from the same warrens. Because rats are invariably found in these places, it is essential that working dogs are inoculated against leptospirosis, or 'rat disease'. Of course, rats will sometimes be found lurking in rabbit warrens out in the cleanest of country areas, so this inoculation should be given as standard when the dog is a puppy, along with the parvo and distemper vaccinations.

While ratting in Nottingham at a farm where chickens and geese were kept free-range at the side of the farmhouse, the dogs entered a field of kale and began marking eagerly at a pile of tree branches and exposed roots; we decided it must be full of rats. Carl Noon entered his polecat jill, a superb rat- and rabbit-hunting ferret, and she quickly disappeared after the telltale bushing and jerking of her tail – and it wasn't long before a rabbit came hurtling out of the woodpile and quickly disappeared into the long rows of crops, with the pack of yapping, excited terriers in hot pursuit. Carl's jill emerged, then turned and re-entered the lair and another rabbit was quickly bolted, and then a third, along with a large rat which, unlike the rabbits, didn't wish to take its chances out in the open. It needn't have worried, though, for the dogs were away in the distance, searching the kale for those fleeing bunnies. Rats are quite regularly bolted alongside rabbits, especially in crop-growing areas where they are far more plentiful.

gamekeepers in their efforts to control rabbit numbers. Tenant farmers suffered problems from these large colonies of coney, and so keepers had to attempt to keep their numbers within sensible limits. Snaring was one of the favoured options, as it took far less time and effort than other methods, time that could then be spent on other, more important duties. Poachers too, have used snaring to great effect, for this is a silent and swift way of taking rabbits, and far less risky than ferreting and running them with dogs. The only trouble was, if a keeper discovered a snare, very often by accident as he patrolled the estate, all he had to do was hide somewhere nearby and wait for the poacher to return in order to check his trap, catching him in the act and securing a conviction, or meting out his own justice in ways already described.

Avoid the Working Railway Line

Never hunt rabbits alongside, or anywhere near, a working railway line. I have done so in the past, and have had a couple of close calls whilst doing so. The Bury to Manchester line cuts through some rough ground that is well populated with rabbits. Many years ago, a few friends and I would hunt these grounds frequently, and many times the lurchers would be chasing rabbits all over the place while a train went whizzing by, the startled faces of the occupants framed in the windows. Two of these friends, Ian and Graham, owned shotguns, and they would shoot the rabbits bolted by my ferrets. They never bothered with actually gaining permission, so it is quite likely that the shotguns were without licence, too.

One of my 'close calls' was when we

Rocky and his daughter, Sadie, chasing a rabbit all over the place. Stay well clear of roads and railway lines!

decided to take a short cut after ferreting this rough ground, actually walking alongside the lines towards Bury in order to get back to the canal side by climbing through a convenient hole in the fence. But Merle, my lurcher, went on to the track and touched the live rail. He suddenly yelped with pain, and then so did Pep, my Jack Russell terrier: she, too, had strayed on to the live rail, and screamed in agony. Instinctively I reached out to pull them off, not thinking it through that I would be electrocuted too; but fortunately for me the electric pulse threw the dogs off the track, and I avoided what could have been a fatal shock! Furthermore, if a train had come along at top speed while we were walking alongside the track, we would have had no chance of getting out of the way.

These were certainly rich rabbiting grounds, but from that day forward I have avoided them at all costs.

Another Close Encounter

Another close call was when I was hunting an area known as The Burrs, a charming area of a small wood and rich green pasture, cut through by the River Irwell. A railway line also cuts through this land, ending at Rawtenstall to the north. In those days the line, although still used by diesel engines, was frequently out of use and the embankments made excellent hunting grounds. In fact, the whole area was teeming with rabbits in those days. Quite a number are still found today, but after a severe outbreak of myxomatosis a few years ago, they have never recovered in quite the same numbers. I spent many fruitful days in this part of Lancashire, and took many rabbits with my ferrets and dogs.

On this particular day we were ferreting the embankment while the rest of our poaching gang stood in the field with the lurchers on the slip, ready for any rabbits getting through the purse nets. Also, there were quite a number of bramble thickets along this embankment, as there still are today, and so many bolt holes could not be netted. Invariably, rabbits will bolt from those holes that cannot be covered with a net, and so at least a brace of running dogs were necessary.

We were moving up to the next part of the embankment to be ferreted, crossing a bridge that was very narrow indeed. In fact if a train came along, there was no room on the edges to get out of its way, so if you stood your ground, then the porter in Bury, just a few minutes later, would be scraping you off the front of the train with a shovel! Of course, a train *did* come along when we were on that bridge, and we had to make a very quick decision: in unison, we all turned and ran. Pete, a friend of mine who was very athletic and well known as a fast runner at school, was in front, but I can tell you I had no trouble keeping up with him as I heard that train thundering down towards us.

Another thing I noticed was that the driver made absolutely no attempt to slow down, just as though he had decided to leave our fate to chance. A large bramble thicket grew at the edge of this bridge, and we all leapt over it just in time, as the train came speeding past. We were all shaken by the experience, and from then on passed over that bridge very rapidly indeed. Shortly afterwards the line fell into disuse, and so we had nothing to worry about. Nowadays, however, this line is used by the East Lancashire Railway Company, which runs steam locomotives from Bury to Rawtenstall; at the time of writing it can often be seen in the BBC television drama, *Born and Bred*.

Rabbiting on Motorway Embankments

Motorway embankments are often full of rabbit warrens – but again, *never* fall to the temptation to go hunting there. I know of some who have actually hunted these places, even digging foxes as the cars sped by, but you would be in serious trouble if you were caught, not only for trespassing on such land, but for hunting game. Declan Feeney was not at all choosy about the places he hunted, and if rabbits were found there, would hunt them, including railway and motorway embankments. I have known Dec hunt rabbits in the gardens of country houses, too – but more of that a little later.

A Heart-Stopping Hunt

My lurcher also once had a very close brush with disaster involving a motorway. There is a small patch of land by the M66 that is surrounded by busy roads. It is almost triangular in shape, and on all three sides there is a constant stream of traffic. The M66 runs along one side, the slip road along another, and a busy main road runs parallel to the motorway on the third. I don't hunt this area any more, but when I was just a lad I took many rabbits from this place, for it was overrun with them. Part of this area is in the grounds of a large country house, but the gardens were rather unkempt and the undergrowth afforded shelter to hordes of bunnies.

There were quite a few warrens along the hedgerows here, and a particular favourite was one that led into a small land drain: the dogs always marked eagerly here. It was no different on this particular day, with both Merle and Pep digging at the entrance. I quickly stopped them, because the last thing we wanted was for the rabbits below to be alerted of the danger outside. I netted the holes, and then entered my polecat jill, Jick, the best working ferret I have ever owned.

This warren was quite a large one and stretched for maybe fifty yards or so, with several offshoots and bolt holes from the main drain, so it usually took quite some time for the action to begin. I sat there waiting while the dogs stood rigidly, trembling with keen anticipation, as cars whizzed by on all sides; and then we could hear the familiar sounds of thumping and bumping, the signal that Jick had her quarry on the run at last. She knew this warren inside out, so there was no hiding place for those rabbits, and eventually they made a bid for open ground. The first rabbit hit the net at lightning speed and was secured. The second, which chose the same hole, flew out immediately after the first and was instantly on the run.

Merle sprang into immediate pursuit of his quarry, straining every muscle as he coursed it across the rough pasture. What followed was one of *the* most spectacular chases I have ever witnessed, and as the rabbit and lurcher headed off along the gradually narrowing strip of green, surrounded now on both sides by the motorway and the slip road, the scene became framed by the unusual backdrop which somehow added to the spectacle and made it even more amazing and exciting. But I began to get increasingly worried as the rabbit headed straight for the motorway, with my lurcher now very close on its heels. Fortunately the combination of the fast oncoming traffic and the closeness of the dog made the rabbit turn completely around so that it was now running in the opposite direction, the strip of green

thankfully broadening again. I shouted encouragement to Merle and he now gained ground once more, finally picking up his quarry close to another warren which it was definitely going to use as a means of escape.

It was a superb course and catch, but it must rank as *the* most heart-stopping hunt I have ever witnessed. I had never before thought of the dangers associated with hunting such land, but they were quickly brought to mind on that sunny autumn morning when I feared I was going to lose Merle on that motorway, and all for the sake of a rabbit! I have been far more careful since!

Shortly afterwards I met a man with a lurcher who told me of his experiences with motorways. There is a stone drain on the edge of a golf course that sometimes holds foxes; I often checked it myself in those days. He had put a terrier to ground, and the constant baying soon confirmed that Reynard was at home. The fox bolted and a lurcher was slipped, quickly gaining ground on its quarry, which slipped under the fence and, to his horror, ran on to the M66. The lurcher was right on top of its fox by this time, and both fox and dog died together as a car hit them at speed. Running dogs close to motorways, or indeed, busy main roads, is not recommended.

As an example, John Settle of Todmorden once flushed a fox close to the 'Owd Bets moors, and it ran across the busy road that cuts through this weather-beaten landscape, linking Edenfield and Rochdale, making it to safety. Alas, the poor terrier was not as fortunate and was killed as it followed its quarry. John was unlucky, for this area has miles and miles of barren wastes where the fox could have run, but it chose to cross the road instead.

Derek Webster and Chris Dewhurst with Rocky and Sadie, in typical northern rabbiting country.

Scores of lurchers and terriers have been killed on busy roads. I have had some close calls, but luckily have escaped without losses. I take much more care these days, and never hunt too close to a road.

Rabbiting on Sand Dunes

Sand dunes are another fruitful place for the rabbit hunter to visit. Not only do the sweet grasses that grow in such areas provide plenty of nourishment for a thriving rabbit population, but the ground is very soft and so it takes little effort for warrens to be dug out. The sand dunes on North

Uist are full of rabbits, and Tim Green runs his Plummer terrier pack at them here; I visited these dunes when I was on the island, and it was very exciting watching this pack at work. Jack and Mask were the main leaders, and they busily cast around, constantly searching for their quarry and putting up rabbit after rabbit. These were then chased and hunted over the dunes, but the quarry invariably escaped by getting into one of the many warrens dug deep into the sandbanks.

Tim had left his ferrets at home that evening, for we were just enjoying a stroll while the pack worked excitedly; so these rabbits were left for another day. I was

41

Tim Green's Plummer terrier pack.

The pack hunting on Uist.

most impressed with these busy, hard-working terriers; their instinct to pack, brought about by the inclusion of beagle blood, meant that it was like watching a mini pack of hounds at work. Their striking colour also means that they stand out and are easy to follow whilst at their work, and this made the whole scene even more enchanting, of moorland and mountain, of miles of open grassland, and of the beach front with the swishing foam of the sea-shore, standing out starkly against the darkening backdrop of the western sky.

Seeking Permission to Hunt Rabbits

Poachers, of course, don't bother about gaining permission to hunt rabbits, or any other game for that matter, and I have done more than my fair share of poaching in the past; but nowadays I always seek permission on the places I hunt, and this is by far the best policy.

Gaining permission is not always easy, but the effort is well worthwhile, for you are bound to be successful at some farms. The most important aspects of seeking permission are always to be polite and well dressed. When asking for permission, stress that you are there to carry out a *free* pest control service, and that the farmer would be welcome to have some of the catch for himself, ready skinned and gutted, or otherwise, should he so wish.

You must also make it quite clear that you will not disturb livestock in any way, and will show the utmost respect for property such as fences and walls. And make it clear that you would be quite prepared to help out in times of emergency.

Once you have gained that permission, make sure you value it, and never abuse

the kindness of the farmer by leaving litter or damaging fences or stone walls. By showing respect in this way, and a willing attitude if your help is needed, you will undoubtedly continue to enjoy that permission for years to come. For example, on several occasions I have been able to show a farmer that allowing me on to his land was to his direct benefit, not only because of the fact that I am ridding his land of a serious pest, but also because I have been helpful in other ways.

One of these occasions stands out as a time when I went beyond the call of duty, and my actions mean that that permission is mine more or less for life. I was hunting the high ground deep into midwinter and had been tramping the moors for quite a few hours. The rabbits up here are far wilder and harder to catch than their low-land cousins, and the terriers had been hunting them among the large number of reed-beds of this area, often flushing snipe as they did so. These flew away across the heather-clad landscape at a rapid pace, and I could readily understand why many hunters enjoy shooting this bird: they are incredibly quick and turn from side to side in an often zig-zagging flight which makes them a near-impossible target.

Helping in Emergency Situations

There is an old quarry on the edge of these moors, and several rabbits skulk in the rockpiles here. I entered the quarry and immediately noticed a sheep on a narrow ledge on the crag face, obviously stuck: it had jumped down from above, but its back hoof had become trapped fast in a narrow cleft in the rock, and it was unable to move as I approached. It was a Swaledale ewe, and she was in serious trouble. I needed to

Heading on to the moors.

lift her so that I could get the back hoof clear of the cleft, and I did this by hooking the end of my walking stick around her neck, and lifting at the same time as I lifted her leg. The only trouble was, this was a narrow ledge and we were quite high up; piles of rock and scree lay below this crag, and if the sheep panicked once she was free, that was where the pair of us would land.

I dug in my heels as I lifted the foot free and kept a firm hold on her leg, the stick hooked around her throat, a little apprehensive at what would happen next. But I needn't have worried. Perhaps animals sense when you are trying to help them, because she allowed me to drag her off that ledge and to safety without even flinching. I left her on safer ground and went to inform the farmer, and I felt I immediately grew in his estimations.

On another occasion I was again able to help a farmer who had given me permission to hunt his land. We had been hunting among hilly pastures at a place known

locally as 'The Tops' and had caught two rabbits. One was taken from a stone wall after it had shot into a gap in the stones when hard pressed by my greyhound Bess. In the next field another rabbit exploded from a grass tussock, and Bess coursed it eagerly. The rabbit was game, however, and put in a few good turns before the inevitable end came.

On the way home we had to cut through a nearby farm, and there I could see Trevor, the farmer, waving to get our attention. It was obvious something was wrong, and of course we immediately responded. We walked up the small valley and found Trevor with a cow that had somehow stumbled into a fast-flowing brook. It was still well and truly winter, and the icy water tumbled down from the frozen moors above; a frost, hard in places, still lay on the ground, despite this being late morning, and a cutting wind swept down from the icy wastes far above. That cow had been stuck fast in the brook for quite some time, and it was a matter of urgency that we got her out of there. Hill cattle are hardy, but few animals could last for long in those icy waters, for she was off her legs by this time, and was lying in the water. The brook was quite narrow and so, once down, she could not manage to get back up again. I suspect that one of Trevor's little Lancashire heelers had chased her, causing the cow to lose her balance and fall into the stream. Lancashire heelers are quite a rare breed, and are so named because they have been used for hundreds of years for helping to bring in the cattle at milking time, nipping stubborn beasts in the heel. Trevor kept a small pack of these dogs, together with a few Jack Russells, to help keep down the rats, and one of them was obviously exercising this in-bred instinct. The trouble was, that particular cow did not belong to him, but to the neighbouring farmer, Noel.

Barry, my hunting partner, Trevor and myself attempted to lift the cow so that she could stand on her own again, but she was too heavy for us. It was decided that I should go and find Noel, which I did, and we hurried back to where the cow was fast losing her fight against the chilled winter torrent. I went into that icy water up to my knees, and after quite some effort we got her on her feet and up the steep bank. But the effort and discomfort were well worthwhile, because we had undoubtedly saved the life of that cow, one of Noel's best milkers as it turned out, and both Noel and Trevor were extremely grateful. I still continue to hunt their land, and undoubtedly this episode has helped secure that permission for so many years.

Yet another episode involved a late spring lamb that had fallen into a deep ghyll out on the high Pennines. Bare rock and shale littered the banks and there was absolutely nothing to graze, so it was imperative that the lamb, being fattened for the sales in November, was rescued and restored to grassland as soon as possible. I climbed down into the ghyll and managed to catch the surprisingly agile bundle of wool, and lift it out on to the rough hill pasture above.

In all these cases the stock animal's life was saved, and the farmer I hope realized the benefit of allowing a rabbit hunter to roam over his land. So never miss an opportunity of demonstrating that it may be in the farmer's best interests to have you on his land, and always show a willing attitude whenever your assistance is needed. If you are around at milking time, or when sheep or cattle are being driven to fresh pasture, show willing and offer your services. Sometimes all that is needed is for you to stand in a gateway or at the entrance to a country lane, in order to prevent the livestock from going down that route. Remember, actions always speak louder than words!

Rabbiting over the High Moors

Some of the most exciting action when hunting rabbits can be enjoyed out on the wildest part of the moors. Often these colonies are fairly isolated, and are incredibly hardy, wild, and resistant to disease. Also, they are a readily available form of some of the best organic meat around, totally free of any contaminants, for obviously no chemicals are used in these remote, untamed regions. These rabbits tend to have very dense fur and this, obviously, is due to the area in which they live, for the moors are often chilly even in midsummer, when the land below is being baked hard and dry. In winter, the temperatures drop

Sadie looking for moorland rabbits.

Moorland rabbits can be difficult to catch.

Jack Webster with Rocky and Gyp – hunting rabbits on the moors.

rapidly, and snow and ice can be found while the lower dales are enjoying much milder conditions.

Moorland rabbits are far wilder and harder to catch than lowland rabbits: they are constantly harassed by foxes, badgers, stoats, buzzards and owls, and so are highly alert. Many are found below ground, often in warrens that cut through the peat and lead into rock crevices; places where all predators, excepting stoats and ferrets of course, just cannot get to them. Some of these rabbits will feed far from their warrens, due to the fact that food is much harder to come by, and much more travelling is involved in their search for goodies, and some great runs can be enjoyed with lurchers in these circumstances. In woodland and on pasture, rabbits roused above ground will usually have a 'short burst', but will soon have reached an underground lair, leaving a lurcher staring into the darkness, a picture of frustration and often bewilderment.

The moorland rabbit, however, will have quite some distance to cover before reaching its more traditional home and so a good, long run will ensue, with the rabbit craftily using any and all obstacles on the way. Reedbeds and deep heather will be used in order to throw off the pursuer, and often to great effect. Terriers too, will chase these rabbits, and it is great fun watching these little bundles of energy and belligerence as they twist and turn among the reedbeds, constantly attempting to catch the fast fleeing quarry. These attempts almost always fail – except, that is, when myxomatosis strikes.

My terriers have caught rabbits among the cover of the reeds, but usually they are diseased ones that need putting out of

their misery. However, on the higher parts of the moors where more isolated colonies of rabbits are found, I have never come across myxied rabbits. This may be due to colder temperatures hindering the onset of disease, or because these colonies are completely separate from their lowland cousins; maybe they are completely immune. I do not pretend to know the answer, though I guess it is probably due to a combination of the first two theories; I can only speak for the areas I hunt, mainly among the Lancashire moors. Myxied rabbits may well be found on the moorland of other areas, but this is probably because none of the rabbit colonies in these places are isolated, but run one into the other. This is so in North Yorkshire, where myxomatosis has broken out on several occasions during recent years, though the population hardly seems dented by these outbreaks.

A good-sized rabbit taken from moorland.

Terriers hunting rabbits on the Lancashire moors.

A Moorland Hunt in North Uist

One of the most exciting of moorland hunts I have taken part in was when I visited Sue Rothwell and Tim Green at their North Uist home. Tim and I set forth over moorland and mountain, and these areas are vast indeed. We spent hours walking among this wilderness and witnessed some fantastic sights: herds of truly wild red deer at the foot of the mountain ahead of us and just beginning to ascend its slopes, keeping a constant eye on both us and especially the pack of dogs we had with us; and a pair of golden eagles soaring high above as they scanned the landscape below for a potential meal. A lone woodcock would explode from the ground in places and go flying across the heather at a rapid pace, heading to some other remote hideout. The terriers caught many voles as we crossed that land, and this was encouraged by the owner of that estate, for voles nibble the young shoots of sprouting trees and quickly destroy them. There

were few trees on Uist, and that is very much due to the large rabbit and small rodent populations in this area of the Outer Hebrides. At the side of a loch, in the middle of nowhere and far from any pasture or cultivated ground of any sort, the pack of dogs began hunting keenly and for a minute or two we believed them to be hunting the line of a mink.

The pack of Plummer terriers then went to ground under overhangs of peat and heather by narrow watercourses, and eventually began yapping and baying, signalling a find. A little later, a rabbit bolted from out of the overhang and ran along the edge of the loch, before disappearing in the deep heather. The pack hunted its line for a while, but it soon became obvious that the rabbit had made good its escape.

This has to be the wildest and bleakest spot I have ever visited, with not a sign of any decent grazing anywhere nearby; yet that landscape still held rabbits. Not a large colony, true, but rabbits could still survive here, even if it was in low numbers. Because rabbits live in such isolated pockets, as they do on the Lancashire moors, they often escape outbreaks of myxomatosis. If rabbits were introduced into these colonies from other areas, then the consequences could be very serious indeed, even wiping out these small populations as they would have no immunity to the strains being introduced; another reason why it is best to avoid such practices, allowing an area to recover naturally after an outbreak of this terrible disease.

(Pages 50-52)
Derek Webster and
Chris Dewhurst
controlling rabbit
numbers in the
Dales.

Summary

To summarize: rabbits can be found almost anywhere, from wasteland in and around towns and cities, to the bleakest of moors. Permission is not easy to gain, true, but with persistence, the rabbit hunter will find success at some very good locations. Derek Webster of Rochdale gained permission at a farm where trees were to be planted extensively. The owner had been given a grant in order to help finance this planting scheme, but on the condition that rabbits were kept under control, for they can destroy young trees by nibbling away at the bark. Derek helps control the numbers and he has to fill in forms to say how many he has taken. Such land is only dreamt of by most rabbit hunters, but there are many fruitful hunting grounds out there, it just takes a little time and effort to find them!

CHAPTER 4

OF FERRETS, LINERS AND LOCATORS

While there are several different ways of bolting rats, there is only one really effective way of bolting rabbits from their underground burrows, and that is with ferrets. This slender, game member of the weasel family has been used for millennia rather than decades, and so has an ancient association with man. The Romans certainly kept ferrets, and used them to flush rabbits from warren systems similar to those used by the Norman conquerors; some people have even suggested – incorrectly in my opinion – that it was the Romans, rather than the Normans, who

Ferrets: the only effective way of bolting rabbits.

A sandy jill ready for work.

first introduced rabbits to the British Isles. Whoever it was, it was the rabbit poacher who has made the most use of the ferret. When I was a lad, several folk on and around the estate where I grew up kept ferrets. All poached, and the rabbit meat was either sold to a not-so-choosy game dealer, or was used to help feed the family.

All one hears about nowadays, especially from ferret welfare groups, is how these ferrets were kept at the bottom of gardens and almost left there to rot in small cages with dirty water and not enough food. While this may be true in some cases, I am bound to defend many of these ferret keepers, who looked after their charges well. Although some may have been kept in quite small rabbit hutches, most had large cages with plenty of room. Some were kept in a cage inside a shed, and these were allowed out and were able to exercise throughout the space of the shed floor. They were worked regularly, too, so boredom was never an issue,

and they lived mainly on rabbit meat, particularly heads and innards such as liver, kidneys and heart. So disregard tales by ferret welfare extremists who complain about how ferrets were kept in the 'dark days' before their organizations came on the scene, for much of it is nonsense: ferrets in those days had a good life, and with more than enough good quality food to eat.

I don't wish to gainsay ferret welfare organizations altogether, because on the whole they do a superb job; but most rabbit hunters of former times, myself included, cared deeply for the welfare of their ferrets, and made sure they were happy and well. Besides, it pays to do so, because a contented, healthy ferret will earn its keep by giving a good day's work. An unhealthy ferret, on the other hand, would fare badly at work and would spend much time lying up, whether it had made a kill or not, unable to resist a warm rabbit bed! Unhealthy ferrets are lethargic and give a poor account of themselves in the hunting field, so few serious hunters would neglect such a vital member of their team.

One of these rabbit hunters kept his ferrets – two polecats, as I remember – inside the garden shed, and they were free to roam around it, with a ramp from the cage leading down to the floor; so they had plenty of room for exercise and play. Mick hunted with them, and certainly on our estate they had a reputation for being vicious, though this was said of any ferret in those days. Even now, when much has been done to raise the profile of the fitch family, many people continue to associate savage bites and huge leather gloves with the keeping of these animals. This was in the early days of my ferret keeping, when I didn't have a great deal of confidence in handling them – and hereby hangs a tale. One night after a poaching expedition we returned to discover that we were locked out, and the only place to shelter was in the polecats' shed. But we were both terrified of these polecats, and stood at the unlocked shed door, trying to summon the courage to go inside, pick up the 'savage' pair and secure them in their cage, so that we could bed down there for the rest of the night.

The whole night had in fact been a complete disaster. Dec was using his bitch Cassy, and I had agreed to do the lamping for him. We were hunting some big fields close to the farmhouse, but were not worried, for the night was pitch black and quite windy; near-perfect conditions for lamping rabbits. Despite this, however, we had come across few sitters, and most of the rabbits had been quite near their warrens, so they quickly disappeared below ground, leaving us, not to mention the lurcher, rather frustrated. Not to worry. The land we were now lamping was well populated by rabbits and was quite exten-

sive, so there was much to go at. Surely we would find more success here!

We entered a big field containing a large herd of cattle, though we didn't see them until the lamp swept across and picked out the black and white Friesians. This was rich pasture of the highest quality, so could easily support such a large herd; but the farmer would not be too happy about us tramping across his land. These thoughts went racing through my mind as the cattle started to look unsettled. They would soon be taken in and housed for the winter, and it was unfortunate for us they were still running out, because they took the dog to be a major threat and began charging us. Normally I will see off any cattle that show signs of going after my dogs, but this was in the middle of the night and the herd was extremely large. As they thundered across the field heading straight for us, with one accord we turned and fled. At the first sign of danger Cassy had summed up the situation and quickly leapt over the high wall to safety. Dec was of an athletic build and he, too, was rapidly over that wall. I, however, had a heavy battery and lamp hanging around my neck, so it took a few attempts as I tried to get a grip on a jutting stone in order to pull myself up. I caught the flick-switch on the lamp a couple of times and the beam illuminated the farmhouse, shining straight into the bedroom windows. Dec was almost screaming for me to turn it off, but I was more concerned with getting over that wall as the cattle were now almost on me. I made it just in time, but surely half of the country community had been woken and alerted by now!

Having reached the safety of the next field I composed myself and turned off that powerful light – when a loud blast from a shotgun rang out into the night and almost deafened us, it was that close. We almost jumped out of our skins and the dog nearly abandoned us: we didn't need any more warning fire, I can tell you, and quickly turned tail and ran for all we were worth. The trouble was, the switch on the lamp kept catching my leg as I ran, flicking the light on and off, so the farmer could easily inform the police of the way we were heading. A couple more blasts from the shotgun rang out, but we were now well away from the farm and so began to slow down to a walking pace once more.

Just as we were beginning to relax and contemplate where we would go next, a police car suddenly turned on to the golf course below and the headlights swept across the well manicured turf in our direction. Panic stations once again. We began running once more and, yes you've guessed it, the switch caught on my leg several times and the beam clearly lit up our escape route. Dec was now running for all he was worth and I was struggling to keep up with him – though by this time I had realized that if I just turned the lamp around we would have no further problems with the beam flicking on and off.

That had all happened an hour or so ago, we were exhausted, and now sought a rest for the night in Mick's shed. The fearsome tales about those ferrets turned out to be false, and the two proved easy enough to handle as we bundled them into their cage and lay out on the floor. The place, as you can imagine, smelt strongly of fitch, and Dec's snoring added nothing to the overall 'charm' of the place, so in the end I decided to move digs and went round to a friend's house where I slept in the porch. All in all it was one of the coldest night's 'sleep' I have ever had, and I would not wish to repeat the episode.

Acquiring Your Ferret

Some people will warn you against ferrets that are bred from pet stock, but in my experience it matters little how a fitch is bred. Domestic ferrets, whether of working stock or otherwise, still retain a strong hunting instinct, which is readily aroused when they are put to work. I have entered ferrets from pet stock, and have also purchased adults that have been kept just as pets and have then begun working them, and have found them to be almost as good as working stock. Some ferrets from working stock have taken quite some time to catch on, while others have entered quickly, some immediately. The pet stock has been similar, though there may be a case for these taking a little more time to enter. Ben was certainly kept as a pet and took an age to catch on, but not all pet-bred ferrets are difficult; some enter very quickly indeed, like working stock, and make superb workers. Of course, there is always a small percentage that makes very poor workers, and some may even refuse to enter at all, but that can be said of both pet and working stock. My advice is, if there are working ferrets in your area and you can purchase from working stock, then do so, but do not be put off if you can only find ferrets from pet stock.

There are also ferret welfare societies that take in many lost and unwanted ferrets, and provided they are not 'anti' working ferrets (yes, people with such principles do exist), some excellent workers can be obtained. In fact adults from welfare societies are an especially good option for those seeking to purchase a fitch, for the owner of the establishment will make certain that you get a friendly non-biter, and they may also know of the working ability of such a purchase, making certain you obtain a 'little cracker'. Those who run these welfare centres are always glad if they can place their charges in good homes.

Ferret kits are ideal for the beginner, but when looking for a worker I would not rule out an adult that is for sale, provided you consider it 'with your eyes open': for instance, if the seller has huge leather gloves on when handling it, then obviously you should not even consider such a purchase. But if, on the other hand, the seller can clearly demonstrate that the ferret is amenable and easily handled, and that it is healthy and obviously well cared for, then if the price is right, go ahead and make your purchase. Even when I had little experience of handling and working with ferrets, I purchased some really good adults that proved excellent workers.

Starting with Kits

Starting with kits has many advantages. For one thing, plenty of gentle handling and play as they grow will enable you to rear a trustworthy worker that will not grab your finger every time it emerges from a burrow. Also, your fitch will be unspoilt: there is always a risk when purchasing an adult ferret that it may have been handled roughly and is a 'skulker', one that rushes back into a burrow every time you reach for it. This is a most annoying habit and can cost a great deal in time if you have to keep making an unsuccessful grab for it.

In the end, all one can do is put a dead rabbit at the entrance, and once the fitch has latched on, pull it free of the hole; but again, this takes time, and once done, you have to wrestle with the fitch in order to get it to release its grip on the rabbit! This is a 'no win' situation and one that is easily avoided by starting with a kit. When a ferret emerges from a hole, simply reach out and lift it up gently: gentle handling will always produce a fitch that can be picked up, once a warren has been thoroughly covered.

It is best to start with kits.

One of the best advantages with purchasing a kit is that it can be reared with a puppy – if you will be using a rabbiting dog, that is – and the pair can be trusted to work alongside each other. If you already have an adult dog, then provided it is well broken to ferrets, the kit can grow up in close proximity to its hunting partner and will then be trustworthy with dogs. On many occasions I have seen ferrets shoot out of a warren or a rat hole, and attempt to latch on to a dog standing nearby. If reared with dogs from a young age, a ferret will not do this.

Thus rearing kits is a good way of starting and comes highly recommended, but I still do not rule out the purchase of adults, as long as they are easily handled and in good condition. I have enjoyed much success both with kits, many of which I have bred myself, and adult purchases. True, some were better than others, but I have not yet had a ferret, either pet-bred or from working stock, that would not 'go' in the end. Believe me, if Ben could be 'persuaded' to enter, then there is hope for any fitch out there!

Kits are generally born during the month of May, if artificial lights have not been used. Ferrets come in season during the spring, and the increasing light triggers this 'breeding season'. Some people use artificial lights in order to imitate the increasing daylight of springtime, and succeed in bringing both jills and hobs into early breeding condition; this is no doubt so they have kits large enough for summer shows. There is no harm in this, but I am a lover of natural law and prefer my kits to be born when nature intended.

By September, a kit will be old enough to begin work, and will have few problems handling rabbits, so this is about the right time to enter your young ferret. True, they are inexperienced and may struggle a little at first, but they will soon catch on, and regular work will very quickly make a kit into a good bolter of coney. Wild polecat kits are born at around the same time as domestic stock, and these spend the

Kits can be raised with a puppy.

A kit will be ready for work by early autumn.

summer hunting with their mother. During the early autumn, however, the litter will begin to disperse, and many will be completely independent by this time, though one or two may attempt to remain with the mother until well into the winter.

A Memorable Hunt with Wiswell

One of the best adult ferrets I purchased was a jill that I named Wiswell (the old English name for a weasel). She came with a hob, a son of hers, and the pair were two of the unfriendliest ferrets I have ever come across. They seemed quite happy not to have any human contact at all, and were totally indifferent in my company; thankfully neither ever tried to bite, which was something, I suppose! Nor were they the best workers I have ever had, though

both were competent enough at their work. One of the most memorable hunts with Wiswell was on a large golf course, actually not because it was successful, but because the whole night was a complete disaster.

Graham, Ian, Carl and myself had spent a great deal of time ferreting together using nets, dogs and guns, and by this time we were an efficient unit. Although I engaged in quite a lot of poaching, there were also places where we had permission to hunt, and one of these was a large golf course in Radcliffe. The course was teeming with coney at that time, and the greenkeepers despaired because of the damage the rabbits were doing, even to digging up the greens! Thus it was easy to gain permission at this venue.

So we drew up a plan of action and decided that we wanted to make a big impression immediately. The plan was to lamp the golf course in two shifts; we would take a tent so that two could sleep while two lamped, and after this we would swap, and thus the lamping would go on all night and we would hope that a good number of coney would be taken. At daybreak, all of us would then go ferreting for as long as we could keep it up. We had decided to take purse nets, for the dogs would undoubtedly be too tired to take part in much daytime coursing after a night on the lamp.

A full night on the lamp and as much as the day as possible ferreting, gives the reader some idea of the size of this golf course and of the immense task that lay before us, for rabbit warrens were dug throughout the rough of this course and the ground was honeycombed with them. But it was a good plan, and one that would be vastly effective once implemented, and so we patted ourselves on the back.

All four of us set off for the Radcliffe bus with three dogs, Bess, Merle and Major, a greyhound and two lurchers, and a box with two ferrets secured inside. We also carried a lamp and battery, and a bag full of purse nets, along with the two-man tent that would be our sleeping quarters for the night. We usually walked to these hunting grounds, but it was a long way, and we wanted to save energy for the long hours of rabbiting that we keenly anticipated lay ahead.

The weather wasn't too bad at all when we arrived; it was quite windy, but the cloud cover meant that conditions for lamping would be perfect. The evening was cool, but it was fairly typical early autumn weather and we considered that it should not cause too much discomfort for the night ahead! Having settled on quite level ground at an isolated spot close to the rough, we began erecting our tent. The first

problem was that most of the tent pegs simply bent as we drove them into the ground; we did eventually manage to secure them, but I secretly hoped that a strong wind would not get up. We then discovered that we had left the waterproof flysheet at home, which meant that we would risk getting soaked to the skin if the weather took a turn for the worst. The dark clouds drifting on a slowly strengthening wind, and the damp feel in the air, which cooled rapidly, were rather ominous; but our spirits were high, particularly with the promise of good hunting. The night began to darken rapidly, heightening, if anything, our keen anticipation, and so we prepared for the start of lamping. I connected the lamp to the battery and checked it was working. The battery had been on charge for hours before we set off, and the powerful beam confirmed that all was well.

So all we had to do now was wait until it was fully dark, and then we could get started. We were all going to have a go together for the first hour or so, and then planned to split the night into two shifts; but we would give the rabbits a little time to settle on their feeding grounds before we began. I was using my trusty twelve-volt motorbike battery; once fully charged, it usually lasted for the whole night, or thereabouts.

Thus a little later, with the night now as black as pitch, we emerged from the cramped conditions of the two-man tent and set off to get started. The wind had indeed strengthened, and I could only hope that our tent would still be standing when we returned; but such thoughts quickly evaporated as we arrived at the start of our hunting grounds. A fine drizzle now began to drive across the landscape on the wind, and our hopes of a dry night went with it. I flicked on the beam and swept it across the highly tendered landscape, the narrow light picking out fairway, rough ground, and now and again bunker; but one thing was plainly obvious, and that was the total lack of rabbits on the ground. Another disturbing element that crept into our night's work was the slow fading of the beam, about six or seven hours before it should have done so: our battery had at last outlived its usefulness, and our hearts sank. This was a devastating blow, but there was nothing we could do about it and so we headed back to our little tent for shelter, the rain now falling in a steady stream and the wind rising all the time.

We could not in fact have picked a worse spot for pitching a tent: we were perched on top of a hill and fully exposed to the elements, whereas in among the trees there would be a great deal of shelter. As you can imagine, conditions were a little cramped inside that small two-man tent, with the four of us trying to get comfortable, along with a box of ferrets and three large dogs. We had decided that the best thing to do was to get a good night's sleep and then hit the rabbits hard with the ferrets, purse nets and running dogs at first light, carrying on throughout the day until we had accounted for a good number of them. This, we hoped, would make up for there being no lamping.

The night had now turned really quite nasty: the sides of the tent flapped angrily in the wind, and the rain came down in torrents – at first it ran down the outside of the tent, but with that fly-sheet missing, water began to seep through the thin walls, and the four of us fought to get away from the sides. What is more, the tent pegs were working loose, and the sides of the tent began to fall inwards, right on top of us all. It was the longest and most uncomfortable night I have ever spent – but with the blackness at last fading to a pale grey, it finally came to a welcome end.

We were all tired, cold and a little damp – except, possibly, for the dogs; but all were eager to get on with some real hunting. Wiswell and her son were keen to go, and the dogs were in high spirits – though the same could not be said about us! But still, the rain had stopped, and hundreds of warrens lay before us, giving promise of great hunting to be had throughout the day.

The events of the previous night were already surreal enough, but the day also began to take on a rather strange quality as we ferreted those warrens with absolutely no results. The dogs were not marking, the ferrets were not keen on working the burrows, and nothing bolted when they did. We saw the odd rabbit and even bolted one a little later (the one that got away!), but that was all. The day, just like the night, had turned into a complete disaster.

Later we found out why. Because the rabbit population was so abundant, and also because we had been slow to carry out pest control at that golf course, it had been decided to have them gassed instead: result, no rabbits, and mystery solved. We put the whole episode down to experience and resolved to take care of problem rabbits much more quickly in future!

The Moral of the Story

When seeking and gaining permission, make certain that you set aside time to visit these farms, keepered estates, golf courses, or whatever location is secured, as soon as possible; also, showing your catch will do no harm at all, especially if it is quite numerous. Delaying a visit can only go against your being able to hold on to good permission for any length of time, for no farmer or landowner will have you tramping their property if they feel they are not getting an efficient pest control service in return.

Ferrets and Ferreting

The poacher of rabbits always had a ferret or two handy, and the less scrupulous would pull out their fangs so they were unable to make a kill and thus lie up. A poacher's success depended on a fast, smooth operation, and a ferret making a kill and lying up afterwards would tie a poacher to one area for quite some time, and that time was time completely wasted. Many ferrets were left behind in this situation, especially when a keeper was seen patrolling, or working in that area. Good, even excellent working qualities were always sought by poachers, as a fitch must find and bolt its rabbits

extremely quickly, especially if a gun was being used in conjunction with the ferrets, for the poacher had to be out of the area fairly rapidly if he was to avoid capture. Other less cruel poachers would use muzzles, mostly home-made affairs consisting of string and thin wire. However, to my mind you should *never use muzzles*.

Muzzles, and the Ferret's Likely Antagonists

In my opinion, muzzles should not be used. Rats are often encountered, and very frequently in crop-growing areas, by ferrets working rabbit holes, and one that is muzzled is at grave risk of being seriously injured, or even killed. Rats are aggressive fighters, especially a doe defending her nest. Also, a cornered rabbit can kick with great ferocity, and a ferret's method of self-defence is to climb over the rabbit's back and administer a fatal bite in its neck: muzzled it obviously cannot do this. Foxes, too, are sometimes encountered in rabbit holes,

Poachers wanted rabbits bolted very quickly!

and a muzzled ferret, again, could do nothing to protect itself should a fox stand its ground. True, this situation is extremely rare, for a fox will generally flee from the pungent odour of a fitch; but there is always the chance that one could choose to stand its ground – though it will often quickly change its mind when confronted with an incredibly fast-striking and belligerent fitch. When a fox argues with a stoat over a meal, it is usually the stoat that wins the argument, unless, of course, the fox is very hungry and determined to secure a meal. In the same way, a fox will usually flee from a ferret, as these move with amazing speed, putting even the striking ability of a fox to shame, and bite with immense pressure and savagery.

It is not just foxes and rats, however, that can be encountered by a ferret working its way through the dark tunnel system of a rabbit warren. Rabbits are enthusiastic diggers, and many other creatures benefit from this. The Norman invaders and their descendants, in order to reduce the risk of poaching by the poorer classes, often introduced rabbits to small islands where they were safe from both human and animal thieves. Skomer Island, off the Welsh coast, is a good example of this secure system of 'farming' rabbits, and the animals now found there are descended from those introduced to the island hundreds of years ago. The large number of warrens serves other creatures too, such as puffins, which nest in them during the spring. I was once ferreting along the steep sides of a hidden little valley that held a substantial population of wild moorland coney. Most of the burrows were inside the cracks and crevices of rocky outcrops, and we had taken a few from such places when the dogs began to mark eagerly at another rocky lair.

I pulled them away and entered Jick, my best worker, and typically, she was quickly on her way. But a short time later she began screaming, and I feared greatly for my favourite fitch. I was quite puzzled, though, for the den was far too narrow to allow a fox access, and Jick was a ferocious rat killer, even if she encountered a doe with youngsters; so I began digging as quickly as possible, and eventually uncovering my fitch who had successfully overcome her antagonist. I pulled her out, and sadly, found she had killed a little owl. I am a keen bird watcher, and was sickened to see such a fine looking bird killed by my ferret. Little owls will sometimes use rabbit warrens to seek shelter in, but such an occurrence has only happened to me on that one occasion – thankfully.

Had Jick been muzzled, she would not have stood a chance and that owl would probably have killed her, or severely injured her at best. As it was, she was able to overcome it without sustaining too many injuries. Muzzles are terrible things and serve no useful purpose, except, maybe, when one is breaking ferrets to their working partners: hunting dogs. If a ferret kept striking at a dog, muzzling it and then allowing it to have regular contact with its 'own' dogs may well cure this, though some ferrets will not take to dogs, no matter what you do. In such a situation, all one can do is to keep them away from each other as best you can. Jick was one of those ferrets that would not accept dogs without attacking them; but she still worked alongside several during her six seasons of prolific service.

I know of several people who have bolted foxes with ferrets, sometimes catching them in purse nets. Untangling a live fox from a net is an alarming experience, and many people simply dispatch the quarry before attempting to remove it. This can be done with a heavy blow to the top of the head, though the recommended method is to shoot the fox if one has a gun to hand. I was once ferreting some large pastures up in the high ground close to the 'Owd Bets moors in Lancashire when a fox was bolted by one of my ferrets. The dogs had keenly marked a land drain, a narrow tunnel only eighteen inches or so below the surface, lined on both sides with a few courses of brick and capped with York stone. These drains are all over this area and hold good numbers of rabbits, but exits are found in several different places and so we thought it best to use the lurchers, rather than attempt to cover all escape routes with purse nets.

The ferret was keen to go: I think it was Jick, though it may have been Numbhead, another excellent worker who could clear a rabbit warren in no time, and I took it for granted that coney was at home. I usually used Numbhead for large rock burrows, as these can often take an age for a ferret to work through – but not so with her. She was extremely quick, and was most useful when warrens were larger than normal.

My fitch entered eagerly and soon disappeared into the tunnel. We heard a commotion a short time later, and a hundred yards or so from where we were waiting for the action to begin, a fox exploded out of one of the exits, close to a stone wall, and quickly decided on a route of escape. The lurchers were immediately in action, but the fox had too much of a head start and easily slipped away.

Rabbits and foxes will live side by side quite happily, and so the rabbit hunter may come across a fox inside a burrow more than once, and possibly on several occasions after many years of engaging in this activity; the only worry is how best to deal with it should it become entangled in a purse net. Of course, these nets are far smaller than fox nets and so most foxes will wriggle out of them, but some do become trapped. Others will bolt from an undetected exit and will usually make good their escape, even when lurchers are on 'standby'. Foxes are incredibly cunning creatures and know of the best escape routes long before a ferret, or indeed a terrier, enters their lair, and the exit chosen will almost always be the one that affords the greatest chance of escape.

Stoats and weasels are often encountered too, for these will hunt and lie up inside rabbit burrows; they will bolt just as readily as foxes and will easily slip through purse nets. They bolt so quickly that, nine times out of ten, the dogs will miss them too, very often not even catching a glimpse of them.

The Slow Starter

As already mentioned, some ferrets take a while to catch on to their natural vocation, and a slow starter can be a major cause of frustration to the serious rabbit hunter. However, it is always worthwhile being patient in such circumstances, rather than expecting instant success and getting cross when it doesn't happen. Many terriers that are slow to enter to foxes go on to make superb workers, for they develop at their own pace and only take to their work when they are mentally mature enough to do so.

It is the same with ferrets. A slow starter is usually one that is immature mentally, and not yet ready for 'proper' work. Wild polecat kits develop at different rates, and those that mature more quickly will leave the nest relatively early in the year, and the slower developers much later, sometimes as far on as late autumn, or even into wintertime. I have had a few slow starters, and you will need a certain persistence to enjoy a successful entering programme. Of course, it is easier to enter a fitch than it is a terrier, for ferrets are very much tamed wild animals and the strong hunting instinct that is essential for survival in the wild is still prevalent.

One way of tackling reluctance to enter is simply to keep taking the ferret out and trying it at every rabbit warren that is occupied; eventually its hunting instincts will be aroused and all at once it will begin working. Another method is to use an improvised tunnel system as outlined in the first chapter. Having said all this, even so, a fitch will not usually enter until it is mentally mature enough to do so.

Another method that helps is to feed rabbit meat, with the fur still on of course, to your growing kit. If, however, like myself, you find it impossible to obtain rabbits, simply because you cannot catch them until your ferret enters, then this is not an option – unless you know of someone who hunts rabbits locally and will therefore provide you with a cheap source of meat. Wild polecat jills feed their youngsters on the quarry they will hunt in the future, obviously as an incentive to independence; so when you likewise feed rabbits and rats to your fitch, this will help a great deal when it comes to entering them.

It is debatable whether ferrets that are fed on dry foods are slower to enter, but one thing is certain: ferrets fed on fresh rabbit meat are far more likely to enter quickly because they already know that rabbit scent means food, and a hungry fitch will be much more inclined to search out that food in such circumstances. A young ferret learning its trade should always be worked when it is hungry, even ravenous. True, it is then much more likely to make a kill, but this does no harm at all at this stage, and will give an apprentice a real boost of confidence. If it is worked wearing a locator collar, it is simple enough to dig down to it, and by which time it should have eaten a bellyful and be fully satisfied and content. Your fitch is now well on the way to becoming a seasoned worker.

Entering Jack and Merle

Once Ben had entered and I was enjoying days out with Declan Feeney and other hunters of coney, I was able to feed rabbit meat to my young entries. Jack was one of these, a hob ferret out of Jick and by Bobby, a hob that was worked all over the place by a local countryman who used a Jack Russell – a long, slender, old-fashioned type – to dig out the rabbits his ferret killed below ground: this was long before locators were even thought of. Jack was a handsome animal, but not a large hob like many of the ferrets of those days. Ben was a monster, but most of the hobs back then were huge, for 'liners' were still in popular use when I was a lad, and it was a case of 'the bigger, the better'. At that time we were hunting a beautiful spot near Bolton, a mixture of pasture, pine forest and moorland, with several reservoirs that were popular fishing grounds; it was a place where rabbits thrive.

Many of the warrens there were found close to the edge of the forest, for conies obviously enjoy nibbling not only pasture, but also the bark and young shoots of the trees. In places there were huge grassy mounds several yards in length, that may have been coney beds at one time, used for the harvesting of rabbits by rich landowners who made a fortune out of the fresh meat and dense fur. They were enclosed grounds, and the poorer classes were kept strictly out of them. These coney beds flourished from the time of the Norman invasion of the twelfth century, right up until the wool trade exploded during the eighteenth century, when land was needed for grazing and the enclosed coney beds were abandoned. Rabbits had already escaped from these places and were slowly becoming a serious pest, but the rest were either harvested, or simply turned loose once the trade in sheep had boomed.

The wool trade caused the collapse of whole villages. The village communities were employed at local arable farms, but these were superseded by the booming wool trade, where all that was needed was plenty of grazing and a shepherd. Thus, whole communities abandoned their village for towns and cities, or surviving arable countryside where work could be found. From this time on, the rabbit became a truly wild animal, though many of these coney beds can still be seen today, usually marked on maps as 'giants' graves'. The warrens on the edge of these Lancashire pine forests may well be relics of the past, but they are still very much in use today and I have ferreted them, as did those ancient warreners, on several occasions.

This was Jack's first outing, but being out of my best worker and a first-class hob, he was well bred, besides which he had been fed on rabbit from the day of his weaning, so I was confident of success. I always aim to observe a closed season for rabbiting from the end of February through to late August, but sometimes this is not possible because where rabbits are found in large numbers, the landowners will require your services throughout

the year. Thus the feeding of rabbit meat is possible all year round, though during the warmer months it is important to remove any left-over remains promptly, every day, for fear of stomach upsets, very often fatal in ferrets.

The dogs marked one of these 'giants' graves' and we netted as many holes as we could; there were far too many to be covered by the limited number of purse nets I owned, but we were not too worried about this because we had a brace of running dogs at the ready. These two would course any rabbit that either escaped the nets, or bolted from one of those holes that could not be covered.

Leaving a Ferret Behind

I tried Jack, and at the very first warren he had ever seen, he quickly disappeared below ground. A rabbit bolted shortly afterwards, and then another, and both were coursed by the running dogs: one was caught, and the other was run back into the burrow. Jack did not emerge, however, and it soon became obvious that he had made a kill. Locators were very much in their infancy at this time, and so all you could do was wait until your fitch returned, sometimes two or three hours later. By the time darkness had set in, Jack had still not emerged, no doubt enjoying a long sleep after his hearty meal, and so I was forced to leave him behind. Normally I would have blocked the holes with stones and suchlike, but the entrances and exits to this warren were so numerous that this was impossible. I wasn't too worried about his survival, however, for the place held large numbers of coney and so making a living would not be too difficult for him. Also, because I hunted this area fairly frequently in those

A ferret left behind will cause havoc with keepers' pheasants, or farmer's livestock. Do your utmost to recover a laid-up fitch.

days, I was hopeful of finding him again. If not, then I was sure one of the other rabbit hunters would find him and give him a home, just as I have found the ferrets of others who have lost them whilst rabbiting.

I hate to lose a ferret, but I have lost one or two over the years, during those early days before locators made the finding of a laid-up ferret very simple. Not that I didn't attempt to recover them. I always waited an age for my fitch to return and only left them when forced to do so, either when darkness had set in, or an impatient companion wanted to make a start on the drive home. If possible, I would block my ferret in and return later for it. This was a useful way of handling such a situation, for it meant that I could carry on rabbiting for several hours more, before returning to the warren and unblocking it. My fitch would soon emerge, no worse off for the experience. If, however, a burrow was in

rock, or there were a large number of holes, there would be no other option but to wait. This waiting game could be very hard work indeed, especially if it was raining, or the cold was at its worst during the winter.

Jick killed below and laid up on numerous occasions, though I tolerated this simply because she bolted far more than she killed, and was such an exceptional worker that the occasional inconvenience was a small price to pay. Only once did she push things to the limit, lying up for quite some time while I waited outside in the perishing cold. Normally she would not lie up for long, maybe twenty minutes or so, and would then emerge; but on this particular day she remained below ground for such a long time, about three hours I think it was, that I thought about leaving her for the very first time.

We had been hunting in the shadow of Holcombe Hill, which towers above

Ramsbottom, and the dogs had marked a warren on the hillside. I entered Jick and left the holes clear of nets, for there was quite a bit of open ground where Merle could enjoy a good run, despite the snow on the ground. There was only a thin layer and the ground was as hard as iron with the hard frosts we had been having after the snowfall of a few days ago. A biting north-easterly wind blew down from the Pennines and went straight through the dense layers we had put on, chilling us to the bone.

I entered Jick and, typically, she was soon out of sight, her tail bushing and wagging furiously as she disappeared into the dark tunnel; this was a sure indication of occupancy. And that was the last I saw of my fitch for the best part of the rest of that afternoon. Soon after entering, muffled bangs and bumps sounded from below and shortly afterwards the first rabbit bolted at incredible speed, its paws kicking the snow into the face of the lurcher who now sped after it, close on its heels. The rabbit and dog disappeared over the crest of the hill and I awaited their return, unable to follow, just in case another rabbit bolted, or my ferret emerged. Merle had been loosed in order to give chase, but I still had Bess by my side, lest another coney came hurtling out into the open.

A couple of minutes later Merle returned, carrying the now-dead rabbit back to me. It had been a spectacular run and a long retrieve, and I was very pleased with my young dog, and happy that I had persisted in many hours of retrieve training. The bumping began again, and yet another rabbit shot out of the burrow and headed in exactly the same direction as the other. Merle was already loose and was quickly in pursuit once more. Again, both hunter and hunted disappeared over the

crest of that hill and I awaited the outcome. Once more Merle returned, carrying a now-dead rabbit and retrieved it to hand. Both had been exceptional runs, when one considers the circumstances, for we were in hilly country and the ground was both snow-covered and frozen. The odds were stacked in favour of the rabbit, yet Merle had caught both of them in fine style. I knew then that he was going to make a first-class rabbiting dog.

The waiting game now began, as it became obvious that a third rabbit had chosen not to bolt and had paid the price in full. It was freezing cold on that hillside and minutes soon turned into hours as Roy and I awaited the return of my fitch. By the time three hours had passed, Roy had headed for home, taking the dogs with him and making a bowl of piping hot soup for my return. I was frozen to the bone by now, and could hardly feel my fingers and toes – and for the first time ever I contemplated leaving Jick, despite her excelling abilities at both ratting and rabbiting. I don't know if I have ever been colder than I was on that frozen hillside, and all I could think of was that warm fireside and the hot soup back at Roy's house.

I was about to leave when, thankfully, Jick popped her sleepy head out of the hole. She obviously didn't want to come out into the cold evening air, particularly with a bellyful of fresh rabbit meat, and was about to turn and go back to her warm, cosy nest. I spotted the dead rabbit on the ground and quickly picked it up and placed it at the entrance, moving it about in the hopes of fooling her, making her think it was alive. It worked, and she grabbed the rabbit, and all I had to do then was drag her out of the hole and pick her up. And so finally I gladly headed back to the house where a hot bowl of soup and neat whisky, not to mention a roaring fire, soon thawed me out and had me in high spirits once again, triumphant because of my dog's performance in extremely difficult conditions, and relieved that I had not lost my favourite ferret.

Liners and Locators

Before the days of locators, ferret losses were far more common than they are today. Losses these days are few and far between, but they do happen on occasion, usually when the locator, or collar, fails to work properly and the ferret has made a kill. In the old days, losses could be reduced with the use of 'liners', that is, large hob ferrets which, when not in breeding condition, were rather anti-social and would not tolerate other ferrets in their presence, especially at meal times. They were always housed alone and were not allowed to associate with any other fitch – except, of course, when a jill was to be mated.

Using a Liner

If a jill made a kill below ground, a hob would be attached to a collar and line and entered into the warren. The idea was that the hob would then drive the jill away and she would soon return to the outside world.

To retrieve the hob, two options were now open to the hunter: he could either follow the line and dig down to the rabbit, or he could pull his fitch off the kill and drag it out, thus saving much time. Some would put a knot in the string at 12in intervals and count them as they disappeared, thus knowing how far they would have to dig in order to retrieve their quarry. If only a few feet, then that is what many would indeed do; but if it were several feet, then the only option really was to pull the ferret out. The trouble was that these 'liners' were in peril every time their owner entered them to ground.

A hob ferret used for this purpose – and most hobs were used as 'liners' before locators came on the scene – had to be large and strong out of necessity. Rabbit burrows twist and turn all over the place and the string would soon be dragging on the edge of every turn the ferret made, so the line would become heavier with every one. Tree roots, stones and all kinds of obstacles would be encountered by the lengthening string, and the risk of it snagging was very real indeed. True, in this situation, all the hunter had to do was to dig down to his fitch and rescue it, but some warrens can prove very difficult to dig, and huge boulders can be encountered that completely halt any digging operations.

In this situation, there was no option but to leave the fitch to its fate. Sometimes the collar would snag. For this reason, many skilled countrymen would make a collar, or harness, out of string in order that, should it snag, the string would rot in a short time and easily snap, thus freeing the captive. This was wishful thinking, however, for the ferret would undoubtedly have perished from dehydration long before the string would have rotted. String collars were better, though, for these huge hobs were very strong and their attempts to break free may well have resulted in the string snapping in some cases.

Some would use these line ferrets in rock and the consequences are obvious. Rock holes are veritable labyrinths, and the chances of the line snagging are far higher in this type of warren. I know of someone who, when only a young lad, was asked to use his line ferret at a warren close to the cliff edge in an old quarry. This place still holds large numbers of rabbits, and many can be taken with the use of ferrets, nets and dogs; but rock holes can be bad places to ferret, and the danger of losing a fitch is greatly increased at such venues. The jill had killed below and there had been no sign of her for quite some time.

By late afternoon there was still no sign of her, and so the hob was entered, attached to a string line, and quickly disappeared. The line continued for quite some time, becoming heavier and heavier until finally it stopped: the ferret was unable to drag it any more, and the line simply wouldn't move. The owner attempted to free it by pulling it back, but in the process managed to snap the string somewhere inside. The hob never returned, and the jill, too, was lost; darkness finally forced their owners off the quarry and both ferrets were left behind.

Digging in such a spot was not an option, so one can only hope that the ferret managed to break free and get out. Because of the high risk of snagging and the chances of not being able to dig down to the trapped beast, I for one am glad that the line ferret is now a thing of the past, due, of course, entirely to locators. These devices are invaluable, and make the ferreter's day a much more enjoyable one.

Using a Locator

There may be a few traditionalists out there who continue to use the old system of line ferrets, but such 'dinosaurs' must be rare indeed. Locators can be used in one of two ways: first, by attaching a collar to a jill, just in case she makes a kill below. Countrymen of old always used jill ferrets

initially, for these are much smaller than hobs and rabbits have a better chance of being able to escape their attentions: they will often put up a fight, and have a far better chance of kicking off a jill than a hob. Few rabbits could successfully fight off the attentions of larger hob ferrets, or pass them in tight spaces. Hobs tended to be rather large, when I was a lad anyway – and 'liners' were still very much in popular use at this time – and kills were far more numerous when these were used to ground. Hence jills were the favoured option, and in many cases still are, though kills below are now far less inconvenient because of locators.

Secondly, one could still use a jill to ground without a locator collar on, and if she makes a kill, a hob with a locator collar on can then be entered and the jill quickly located. In this way, hob 'liners' are still in use, though in a much more updated and safer way, a sort of 'twenty-first-century

Locator box and collar.

Rabbit and ferret can be quickly recovered using a locator.

liner'. The only trouble is, the hob may well head for a rabbit that has been killed below, but which had been long since abandoned by the jill in favour of another in a different part of the warren. True, all one has to do is simply remove the dead rabbit and re-enter the hob, but that would mean twice as much digging than would be required if the jill were fitted with a locator collar in the first place.

If, however, the traditionalists out there still want to employ 'liners', then why not do it this way? There is no line that can snag along the way, and a jill that has killed can still easily be recovered, even if more digging will be required. If, for instance, a mark is registered at eight feet or so and the jill has moved on to another rabbit, then one must be willing to dig that depth yet again, if one is going to employ this system. My advice is to use the locator on the initial ferret entered and thus save yourself a great deal of time and trouble. Hobs can still be used, as many are, for bolting rabbits, because kills are not really

that inconvenient when locator collars are used. Gone are the days of standing outside warrens in freezing conditions for hours on end, waiting for that fitch to return. The eating habits of ferrets meant that a lie-up could last for a considerable length of time, and many simply abandoned their charges because of this.

Ways to Prevent a Ferret Lying Up

A ferret will feed for a few minutes at a time and eat its fill, returning to the meal after a sleep; once satisfied, it will once again curl up and sleep. These habits mean that a fitch that has killed below will usually spend quite a bit of time with its kill, alternating feeding with periods of rest – which is why those ferreters of the past who valued their workers, would spend hours waiting for their fitch to emerge.

I was given sound advice in those days, by countrymen who taught me quite a bit about ferrets and their work, which would help combat this inclination to lie with a kill for long periods of time. Upon rising, I was told, feed your ferret and allow it to eat its fill. Bread and milk was no good for this, as a ferret would urinate and defecate almost constantly and saturate its box or bag, and dry foods would make it very thirsty. Raw meat – liver or something similar – was best. This meant that, if the ferret did make a kill later on, it would eat half-heartedly and then come away soon afterwards.

True, after a feed ferrets are quite dozy and will need a sleep. However, they will do this whilst travelling to the hunting grounds, and by the time work comes around, the fitch will be much more lively, though not very hungry. It would then make its kill, have a nibble, and then, no longer being sleepy, would return. I employed this method before locators were on the scene (or before I could afford one!) and it worked, though this method did have its limitations.

I would always be up before dawn in those days, usually long before it started coming light in fact, and so my workers were fed very early on. If they made a kill during the morning the feed I had given first thing would still be effective and my ferrets rarely laid up for long, usually between ten and twenty minutes. However, by the afternoon they would be hungry again, and so many made kills during this part of the day and then laid up for a considerable amount of time. Most emerged after a long wait, while one or two had to be left, very often because darkness forced me down from the hills. So this method was still not by any means foolproof, and locators, therefore, are a real blessing to the rabbit hunter, and make rabbit hunting far more effective and enjoyable.

If, however, you can't afford to buy one, do not despair. You could ask an experienced local rabbit hunter if you could accompany them, and share the use of their locator, contributing towards new batteries whenever they are needed. Your local ferret welfare society will no doubt be able to provide you with details of the locals who work their ferrets (provided, of course, they are not 'anti' working ferrets). Besides, those who believe that ferrets should not be worked without locators are not living in the real world, for a keen youngster is not going to hold back from working his fitch simply because he cannot afford an expensive locator. If you do wish to work your ferret, but do not have a locator, then do so sensibly. First of all, if your fitch does make a kill, ask yourself if you are willing to wait several hours for it to emerge. If you are not prepared to do this, in whatever weather conditions prevail at the time, then you have no business putting a ferret to ground without a locator collar attached.

Also, the policy of feeding your ferret first thing in the morning can be employed. As already discussed, do not use bread and milk, or dry foods: raw meat or liver do nicely as they provide both solids and fluids. Your fitch will then sleep until work begins, and if it does make a kill, as we have seen, will usually emerge soon after because its appetite is already appeased and it is already well rested. However, the chances of it lying up increase greatly during the afternoon, as it will have become hungry again, so it is best to confine your activities to the morning. If you do carry on past midday, then avoid putting a ferret to ground any later than early afternoon; this will allow time for it to return before it gets dark.

If, however, there is no sign of it and the

light is beginning to fade, then block it in, using stones rather than soil, and return for it at first light the next day. By using stones, your fitch will be unable to dig its way out, but will still have enough air to breathe. Using soil is not good because it will either dig its way out, or it will risk being suffocated if it is trapped below ground for any length of time, as soil excludes air. So block exits with stones every time.

If you are either unwilling, or unable, to do these things, then save up for a locator and refrain from working ferrets until you have one. In my view, a locator is now an essential piece of equipment, though

working ferrets in the manner just discussed will greatly reduce the risk of losses, if you can't afford to buy one. And even with a locator, losses do occur, for collars can fail, or batteries can suddenly drain. Sometimes a collar will snap, though checking for wear and tear before use will greatly reduce the chances of this happening.

The Ferreting Dog and Locators

Before the advent of locators, one of the best aides a rabbit hunter could have was a good ferreting dog, for many learned not

A good ferreting dog is a must. (Sadie, owned by C. Dewhurst.)

Rocky marking a warren.

Some dogs have the knack of marking above a kill.

only to mark a warren as occupied (or otherwise), but also to mark above the spot where a rabbit had been killed. Jack, a Plummer terrier I saw at work on North and South Uist in the Outer Hebrides, would do this, and he would also dig into a warren and retrieve the rabbit. Sadie, a lurcher bitch bred out of Derek Webster's superb dog, Rocky, would also mark the spot above where the ferret had made a kill, and she first did this at the very young age of seven months. On this occasion Derek tried the locator where the bitch had begun digging and, sure enough, the bleeper sounded its mark. Many adult dogs will learn to do this, but I have never before heard of such a young dog doing this successfully so early in its training. Lurchers and terriers of such abilities were priceless to ferreters in the days preceding locators – though because of locators they are nowadays less necessary, made redundant by progress, in the same way as the 'line' ferret.

As we have seen, locators have also really made the practice of feeding ferrets before working them unnecessary. That doesn't mean that you can't practise this method, it is just that the benefits for doing so are questionable. One benefit of not feeding is that if you rouse your ferrets a good few minutes before taking them from their cage and placing them in a sack, or carrying box, they will urinate and defecate and thus there will be far less mess whilst out hunting. The only possible benefit of feeding before you go hunting, now that locators have made a lengthy lie-up a thing of the past, is that you may succeed in making your ferret a little sluggish, not quite as sharp as it would be on an empty stomach, and thus kills *may* be less frequent. When ratting, a hungry fitch is always the best option, but when rabbiting this is far less important.

Other Essential Equipment

The hunter of rabbit needs other essential tools as well as the ferret and the locator if he is to carry out effective pest control for

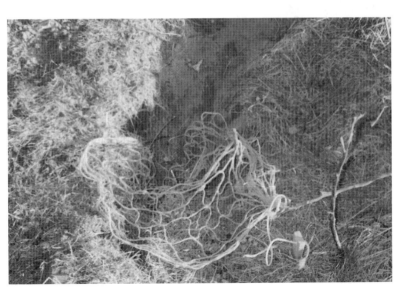

Nets are essential pieces of equipment.

A rabbit caught in a purse net.

those farmers who allow their land to be hunted. Purse nets are the next most important piece of equipment, for serious pest control cannot be carried out without them. Rabbits are amazingly quick and can turn on a sixpence, so catches using lurchers are going to be far lower than those using nets. This is especially true when hunting over rough and rocky ground, such as that found in the Yorkshire Dales. When warrens are on steep ground, rabbits will inevitably bolt and run downhill, giving the lurcher virtually no chance whatsoever of making a successful catch. Nets, in this situation, are absolutely essential (good quality nets can be purchased from the stockists listed at the back of this book).

Another good tip is to have nets of different sizes, for rabbit holes are found in all kinds of different places, and some exits will need a large net to cover them, while others will need smaller ones; so select a variety when purchasing these nets. Some warrens are large, with several exits, so you will probably need to set at least twelve purse nets, though some warrens have far more holes than that. On an average, however, you will have to deal with six to eight holes, so if you have twelve in your bag, then you will have the necessary spares.

A good quality spade will also be needed, for those times when your ferret does make a kill. One with a narrow blade is best, as this is more easily manoeuvred whilst digging down. A pickaxe and such other tools will not be necessary, for rabbit warrens are rarely deep; it is only when a rabbit warren leads into a fox hole or a badger sett that problems may be encountered. It is illegal to disturb a badger sett, and if this does happen – and the chances of this are incredibly small, I have to say – then you would have to wait for your ferret to emerge.

Other warrens may lead into rock crevices in some parts of the country, such as Derbyshire, the Lake District and North Yorkshire, and some of these can be very deep, though they are very often undiggable anyway, so, again, one can only await the return of your ferret in such circumstances. A warren can look innocent in such places, but they can turn out to be very deep indeed and are best avoided the next time you pay your hunt country a visit. On the whole, though, rabbits do not go too deep and a dig of two or three feet will probably work out as the average.

Essential equipment: a good spade, purse nets and locator.

Good quality carrying boxes.

Along with sensible clothing for your-self, and a good quality carrying box, or roomy canvas sack such as those available from listed stockists, and, of course, a decent rabbiting dog (more of them later), these essential pieces of equipment will see you on your way to becoming a sea-soned rabbit hunter.

Gaining Permission to Hunt

What then? I have just spent a day in the Yorkshire Dales with Derek Webster and Chris, his hunting partner; it was a fairly typical day's ferreting. But before we move on to this, I would just like to emphasize that it is always best to have permission

before going ferreting. Permission pre-vents any court action for trespass and being in pursuit of game illegally, and is always the best policy, though I have done my fair share of poaching when I was a lad.

I was out with Declan Feeney and one of his colourful band from his poaching gang, a chap called Neville who had a curious way of teaching his lurcher bitch to put more effort into her running: every time she succeeded in catching a rabbit, he would praise her. On the other hand, every time she failed, he gave her a thrashing. He was what is commonly known as a 'lemon' (of the highest order) and his methods were guaranteed to turn a once bold and fast dog into a quivering, useless wreck. His ways are certainly not recom-mended!

We were hunting the lowlands, which were separated by a broad river. These are rich pastures indeed, and are owned by a dairy farmer who has built up his own dairy products business, which to this day is highly successful. We did quite a lot of lamping in this area, and noticed a great many well used warrens around these fields, and so we resolved to return in order to ferret them. The only trouble was, we had to cross the river in order to get to them and there was no bridge anywhere near. There was nothing else for it: we had to get wet. Fortunately there had been little rain at the time and so our wellies just about kept the water out – though we were not too bothered if we did get a soaking, for those warrens held large numbers of coney and expectations were high. The first warren we encountered was one of the best, and quite a number of rabbits had fled here while we swept the field with the beam during previous visits.

That was under cover of darkness. This was different altogether, for the sunny winter morning meant that we could easily be seen from the farm, which was at the foot of the hill across the large field we were now hunting. Despite this, Jick was entered and all we could do was hope for the best. The nets were not used, for we had two lurchers on duty that day and these were flat pastures and would, we were sure, yield a high success rate of catches.

It was then, as we were listening for the telltale bumpings and bangings from underground, that we heard shouting: a farmer was running across the field, shouting and waving his arms in the hope, I am sure, that we would be sent scurrying back across the river. This we undoubtedly would have done, but I had a ferret to ground, and even Dec had come to appreciate her abilities; so we had resolved to stand firm and take our punishment like men!

The farmer was approaching, and he was in such a rage that his whole head was purple, the large veins in his neck sticking out prominently. He was so angry that he failed to see the rabbits bolt behind him or the lurchers straining at their slips in order to give chase, with Dec and Nev hanging on grimly, not daring to let them go; and he shouted, right into my face, 'Do you?' What on earth he meant I don't know, but we were all asked the same question, and I could see that Dec and Nev were beginning to lose patience. The farmer was small and slightly built, so I have no doubts that he was at grave risk of either Dec, or Nev, or possibly both, giving him a real thrashing and sending *him* on his way. But they kept their cool, by now being wise enough to know that if they took the telling off, they were likely to escape legal action. If they had retaliated, then no doubt the police would have been chasing us all across the country and probably catching us up.

In actual fact we had a simple way of keeping out of trouble: we just gave false names and addresses. Many farmers who caught us on their land just told us to move on, but some became abusive and would take our names and addresses. These individuals fully intended sending the police round, ignorant of the fact that we lived a long way from the addresses we had provided and had never been known by the names we gave!

At last this particular farmer got to the end of his tirade and sent us on our way, back across the river, with false names and addresses noted down in a small writing pad. Once we were on the far bank I waited for Jick to emerge, and then

A working jill emerging from a warren.

slipped back across the water and picked her up, the farmer still walking back to his farm, content now, after venting his anger and frustrations on us!

This experience, and there are others, well illustrates how important it is to have permission when ferreting. If Jick had emerged when the farmer had been there, I am sure he would have confiscated her, though I doubt very much that my poaching partners would have allowed that to happen! Nasty situations are avoided by seeking permission in the first place.

CHAPTER 5

THE USE OF ESSENTIAL EQUIPMENT

Saturday 6 November 2004 was a fairly typical autumn morning. Heavy cloud covered the hills, and at times a light drizzle fell. There was a real chill in the air, warning of the imminent arrival of winter, and the breeze had an icy edge.

We pulled up at the farm not long after daybreak, and the ferret collars were fitted in readiness for the day's work ahead. The ferrets were then put back in their box and we set off, climbing along the track that leads from the village into the hills. These boxes are of the bow-backed variety and are the most comfortable to use.

The start of the day.

Fitting a Ferret Collar

Ferret collars are easy enough to fit, though if the ferret wriggles around it can make the job awkward. Make sure that the collar is fairly tight fitting, not so tight that your ferret struggles for breath, but neither so loose that it risks snagging on anything – a tree root, for example; the ferret may even get a paw caught up underneath if it is too loose. So make sure it is just tight enough.

Personally I prefer to use a sack for carrying ferrets about: these are made of canvas and have brass rings for air holes so the ferret cannot dig its way out. I purchase mine from Arthur Carter Fieldsports (at the time of writing), and these are excellent for transporting ferrets between warrens. I find them less bulky than boxes, and therefore much easier to carry; they are also hard-wearing. With a small wisp of hay or shredded paper in the bottom, they will be suitable for keeping a

fitch for the whole rabbiting excursion – between working periods of course – though they are best cleaned out at the end of each day if they have been soiled. This is unlikely if you have not given a feed to your ferret that same morning, and also if it spends quite a bit of time working, for it will 'soil' inside the warrens it hunts, rather than messing up your canvas sack. During very cold spells you will have to provide extra bedding, whether you use a sack or a box, and two ferrets curled up together will help to keep each other warm.

Nets and Netting

We climbed the hill and headed out on to the fells, with Sadie, Chris Dewhurst's lurcher, immediately marking at a stone wall. Chris could see the rabbit skulking inside and Derek Webster's young sandy jill was tried: she was just entering, and a

Rocky and Sadie marking a stone wall.

Derek entered his young jill.

The rabbit is pulled out . . .

rabbit in a stone wall is an easy and sure find for a youngster. Sure enough, she was quickly on to her prey, and Chris soon had hold of it, dragging it out of the wall and immediately dispatching it. We then carried on and Sadie chased one to ground. A ferret was entered and the rabbit bolted extremely quickly, being secured in a purse net.

Sadie then marked a warren of four or five holes in the bottom of quite a deep ditch, and purse nets were quickly placed over them. When setting these nets, make certain that all the hole is covered. If it is windy, push the metal ring at the bottom of the net into the ground so that it holds it in place, leaving about two-thirds of this ring above ground. This means that it will be held in the wind, but will be easily dislodged by a rabbit hitting the net. Once the net is spread widely around the hole, push the peg into the ground until it is firmly embedded. If the ground is hard, then you may need to use the heel of your boot. The idea is to root the peg so firmly that the quarry cannot pull it free.

The young sandy jill was tried again and she soon disappeared, now a little wiser as to her role in life after working that rabbit out of the stone wall. Shortly afterwards a most unusual event occurred: rabbits will nearly always flee from a ferret at the earliest opportunity, and the two skulking inside the dark passages of this burrow did just that – they burst out of the exit one after the other, and both were enmeshed in the same net!

Derek was on them in an instant, securing them quickly so that the dog did not grab them (a sure way to ruin a good net – and rather unsporting) and making certain that they did not wriggle free. I have seen rabbits get out of nets on quite a number of occasions, so securing the quarry promptly is essential. This also means that the net can be quickly

Derek entered his jill again . . .

. . . and two rabbits hit the net at the same time.

replaced, just in case any others bolt from the same hole – a lurcher is certainly useful at these times, as it will give chase and hopefully catch any rabbits that flee from an unnetted hole.

'Bushcraft'

We moved on, higher up the fells, and one or two rabbits were caught in and around the large reedbeds by Sadie who would stand on point for a few seconds once a sitting rabbit had been located, and then suddenly rush in and either catch or flush her quarry. The mist closed in on us now, as the high tops were covered in low cloud, and it was here that Sadie marked a large warren with several entrances and exits.

In this situation the first thing to do is to net up all the holes as quietly as pos-sible, because even though using a locator means that a ferret killing below ground is nowadays less of a problem, it is still desir-able to bolt as many rabbits as possible – and a sure way of preventing this happen-ing is to make a lot of noise before enter-ing a ferret, because the rabbits will then be nervous about coming out. In fact at one time, before I could afford a locator, I would 'bush' as many rabbits as possible with the dogs, and put as many to ground as I could. Once an area had been 'bushed' I would then return to the first warrens and begin ferreting, as quietly as possible; by then enough time had lapsed for the rabbits to forget about the danger above ground. In this way they were far more readily bolted, and thus far fewer kills occurred, and on many occasions none at all.

Sadie marking a large warren.

Net the holes as quietly as possible.

For rabbits to be so ready to bolt, it is essential to be quiet above ground, and to go carefully whilst netting up. Many people these days, however, do not bother with this, for it is now so easy to recover a laid-up ferret with a locator – which is sad, because the 'bushcraft' element has therefore in many cases been made redundant. Before such devices came on the scene, the hunter of coney would always endeavour to outwit his quarry, and a kill below ground was avoided by any cunning method available. The best is to remain quiet above ground, and allow the rabbits to flee without prior knowledge of danger above ground. Attempting to outwit your quarry is far more exciting than simply going through the motions of pest control in a purely mechanical fashion.

Rabbits will often bolt even when run to ground by a lurcher, and even when a ferret is entered immediately afterwards; but kills will be far more frequent in this situation. I was taught by poachers, who had to ensure that kills did not occur. Declan Feeney would always 'bush' an area first and give the earthed rabbits time to forget their fright before entering a ferret. I have to say that kills in this situation were quite rare, and we enjoyed several days without any of the ferrets lying up.

Dealing with a Large Warren

Once this large warren was netted up, Chris entered his old jill, the mother to two of my ferrets, Socks and Tinker, as she was experienced enough to tackle such a big place. (Young ferrets should be entered in smaller warrens, for these larger places are usually beyond the abilities of a first timer and an inexperienced fitch: leave such warrens to the more experienced.) Collars that had been fitted earlier were checked in order to make sure that everything was working properly. The signal box on the collar was then wrapped in insulation tape in order to keep moisture out, and also to keep it clean. Some people do not bother doing this, but it is always best, for the signal would cease should water get into the electrics.

The ferret soon disappeared, and we waited for the action to begin. This was a large warren indeed, so it takes a little time for the fitch to find, hence the need for patience. Only too often do you see a ferreting man begin sweeping the ground with his locator box a very short time after a ferret has been entered, walking all over the place and alerting the rabbits to the danger outside. It takes time to find in such places, and even then a rabbit can give a ferret the run around for a while, before it either bolts, which is preferable, or jams itself into a dead end and awaits its fate. So exercise a little patience and give your fitch time to work. If there is no sign of either ferret or rabbit after ten minutes, then it is advisable to use the locator box to find where the kill has occurred.

Sometimes a ferret will scratch the back end of a rabbit (and be kicked on a number of occasions for its trouble) in an attempt to move its quarry so that a fatal bite can be inflicted, and it may be feasible to dig down to a still live rabbit. Usually though, if there is no sign of either quarry or ferret after a good few minutes, you can assume the ferret has made a kill. The time you allow between entering the fitch and then beginning the search with the locator box will, of course, depend on the size of the warren. If the place is huge, then allow ten minutes before taking any action, for it takes a while for a ferret to find and a rabbit to bolt in larger places. If it is only a small place with just two or three holes, then maybe three to five minutes will suffice. It is a matter of common sense. The important thing is to give your ferret time to work, and the rabbits the opportunity to bolt undisturbed.

A few minutes later the first rabbit hit the net and Derek was quickly on to it, picking it up, untangling it and then swiftly despatching the quarry. Another rabbit hit the net, and then a third, and both were despatched. Then there was a wait of another few minutes before Chris began sweeping the ground with the locator box. The bleeping sounded, and he placed the box directly over the spot where it was strongest and turned down the dial until he gained a reading. The dial read two feet, and digging operations began, with the murky mist closing in even more and swirling around us. A flock of fieldfares flew across the rocky ground above, and a lone curlew called from somewhere out on the exposed moorland; the occasional sheep bleated on the hill opposite, and these were the only sounds, apart from Derek digging, that could be heard.

Despatching a Rabbit

A humane way of despatching a rabbit.

There are three ways in which a rabbit can be humanely dispatched. The first, and probably the most favoured, is to hold the back legs and then place your other hand directly behind the rabbit's head, stretching it across your hip and thus breaking its neck, as demonstrated in the photograph. The second method is simply to put one hand across the rabbits shoulders and push its head right back with the other. And the third is to hit the rabbit directly at the back of the head, either with a small heavy stick, or with your hand, in a sort of karate chop. All three ways kill a rabbit instantly. The rabbit may kick for a few seconds afterwards and even gasp for breath, but this is simply nerve and brain activity. The rabbit is not conscious at all and is dead as soon as the neck is broken.

Always strive to kill your quarry as soon as possible, and by using one of these humane methods. I cannot stress this enough, for the anti-hunting brigade is determined to ban all forms of hunting, and the rabbit hunter must not give them any grounds for action whatsoever. Respect for the quarry is essential, and in that way cruelty will be kept out of the picture – though, of course, there is a certain amount of cruelty in any form of pest control.

The Art of Digging

When digging, it is important to show respect for the landowner by making as little mess as possible. To begin with, cut out a square of turf and lift it away, making sure it remains whole and intact, for this will be placed back on top of the digging once you have finished. If the depth on the locator reads just a couple of feet or so, then you will only need to remove a small square – the deeper the dig, the larger the square. This is something that is learned with experience: the important thing is to give yourself room to manoeuvre whilst digging.

As you get close to the depth reading, check it again: if you are right on top of your ferret, the dial will be almost at the 'off' position, and you must now go very carefully lest you injure, or even kill, your ferret. Slowly and gently chop through the last couple of inches of soil until the tunnel is exposed, and hopefully the rabbit too, along with your fitch.

You must then backfill the hole and replace the square of turf, leaving as little mess as possible. During the following spring and summer, natural regeneration will obliterate any trace of your having been there. Those who thoughtlessly leave diggings without backfilling them should, in my opinion, be publicly denounced, for this malpractice gives a bad name to all rabbit hunters, and ensures that affected farmers will probably no longer grant us permission, because an exposed dig can be a serious hazard to horses and cattle in particular: if they fell in, either could risk a broken leg, in which case they would probably have to be destroyed. So always make certain that you backfill and tidy the area as best you can. Once a rabbit warren has been cleared, especially if it is located on good pasture, the farmer may even ask you to fill it in, thus reducing the risk of injury to his livestock.

Complying with such wishes is a sure way of cementing relationships and thus of keeping the permission you have

Sweeping the ground and getting a mark on the locator.

Digging down to the ferret and its kill.

gained. Farmers will usually tolerate warrens around pasture, on bankings and under trees, but few will want a large warren out in the middle of a field where cattle or horses are grazed. Another hazard, especially when tunnels are not deep, is the risk of the ground collapsing when large animals are grazing. Again, serious injury can result in this situation, not to mention severe damage to pasture.

Derek dug down a couple of feet and shortly afterwards a dead rabbit was pulled out of the tunnel. The jill had moved on, but soon emerged at one of the exits. The warren was now clear of rabbits and so the backfilling was done, the nets picked up and put away, and we moved on, Sadie keenly hunting the reedbeds and successfully catching two or three more. As we were crossing the reed-covered hillside, Derek suddenly told me to stand still. For a split second I wondered if a snake

was slithering around my ankles, then suddenly he dropped to the ground and grabbed: a rabbit! It was a very determined 'sitter'. I was amazed to see that I had almost stepped on its head, yet it had still not moved! As already mentioned, where rabbits are found in larger numbers, 'sitters' are far more likely.

Store Nets Carefully

When pulling nets up, pull the strings tight by using the metal rings at each end, and then fold, and fold again, finally wrapping the strings around the net in order to hold it in place. By being careful when storing nets between warrens, you will ensure that tangles do not occur, for there is nothing worse than having to untangle every net before you can set them and get on with ferreting; so take a little care, and tangles will be avoided.

Recovering the rabbit.

Chris' jill emerged soon afterwards.

Sadie with a rabbit caught in the reeds.

The rabbit picked up at my feet.

Netting a Hillside Warren

The next warren was on a very steep hillside, strewn with rocks and ridges jutting out of the ground – a bad place for a running dog. This burrow was netted up, as the ground was impossible for allowing the lurcher to give chase, and a couple of bunnies were added to the bag; these were model bolts, straight into the nets. We then moved on, and Sadie chased a rabbit into a land drain. There was no sign of water, but even so, Derek was reluctant to enter a fitch, so Chris put his jill in here, after the nets had been set. She entered eagerly, and could indeed be heard pattering through water; it was hoped that none would get into the collar. After a few minutes it soon became obvious that no rabbit was going to bolt, so a mark was obtained and a depth reading established before we began digging.

When the drain was opened up, we found the rabbit was still very much alive. That drain must have been quite big inside, because the rabbit was clearly giving its pursuer the run around, and kicking her every time she got too close. There seemed to be a shelf that the rabbit kept hopping on, before it was chased off, and then through the tunnel full of water. To cut a long story short, Chris finally succeeded in getting hold of the rabbit and drawing it out, after it had kicked the jill off its back yet again. It was filthy, covered in clay and water; I remarked that it was a 'game 'un' and deserved to run for another day, and since Chris and Derek didn't fancy skinning it in that state anyway, it was allowed to escape.

As it was heading for another burrow, a second rabbit, dry and clean, bolted from the warren and also made an easy escape. However, a little later on another was caught in the reeds by Sadie. And so the day's tally came to an end: seventeen rabbits had been accounted for, most of them by using ferrets and nets, while a few had been caught in reeds – and not forgetting the one caught by the surprisingly agile Derek Webster! Altogether it had been a grand day in the wild uplands of the Yorkshire Dales. The rabbits were skinned out on the hillside, and a hole was dug for the bits that would not be used. This saves having to carry a lot of weight back to the car, and also a lot of work when you get home.

This day out is a model demonstration of how vital equipment should be used – though there is no substitute for experience. We all have our own little ways, but we should all have the following aims in mind: to provide a vital service to farmers who require this pest to be reduced on their land; and to treat the quarry with respect, despatching it as quickly and as humanely as possible.

Derek Webster, Veteran Rabbit Hunter

In the course of this day's work I was impressed by Derek's young sandy-coloured jill with a slight trace of chocolate in its coat; she entered very well indeed, quickly catching on and making rapid progress.

Derek began working ferrets, which he obtained from his brother, at just eleven years of age, and he ratted with them every Sunday. He lived near the River Roche, and in those days pollution was rife, so rats were plentiful. He also ratted at other venues such as knackers' yards, pig pens, sewerage works and tips. There were any number of rats at these places, and large numbers were often taken using ferrets and dogs. Derek used mainly albinos and black-eyed whites in those days, for polecat-marked ferrets were rare in his area, though he did come across the occasional sandy.

Derek's ferrets, like mine and scores of others, were carried in pillow cases and expant legs that had been sewn up at the bottom and were tied with old bootlaces around the top. However, you can't beat proper canvas sacks with air holes, or carrying boxes for transporting ferrets. I personally find carrying boxes too bulky and awkward, but this is probably because the country I hunt contains lower numbers of rabbits than places such as the Dales of Yorkshire, so I have to walk greater distances. Boxes are ideal where there are large numbers of coney, because the walk between warrens is usually only short, but they are less comfortable and so of more limited use when you have to cover miles up and down dale.

Derek learned his trade from an old countryman named Jack Howarth. He kept ferrets and lurchers, and Derek learned much from him – although, as he says, much of what he now knows has been gained from experience and, like all of us, he is still learning. Derek was hunting with Jack after a heavy fall of snow and

Derek Webster, now a veteran rabbit hunter.

the lurchers marked a long drain. The holes were netted and a ferret entered. Jack was watching one set of nets with Jilly, a daughter of Cindy, the lurcher Derek had with him, on guard lest a rabbit escapes the nets. Shortly afterwards a rabbit bolted into one of the nets and Cindy pinned it with her paws, instinctively knowing that there was a chance of it getting out and escaping. Derek approached in order to secure his quarry, but the lurcher bitch growled and bared her teeth menacingly, daring him to go near her prize. Derek turned to Jack – and the old fellow was in hysterics! He had known what would happen, but had decided to set Derek up. Jack then told the bitch to 'leave', and Derek was able to safely untangle his quarry and despatch it. Derek says that the late Jack Howarth of Rochdale was a master of his trade, and he took a great many rats and rabbits with his ferrets and dogs over the years.

Although Derek has hunted many rats in his younger years, he no longer pursues this quarry, having plenty of rabbiting permission to keep him busy. Most of the good ratting spots he used to hunt are now gone, swept away in the fast rising tide of 'progress'. He would never use ferrets for dual-purpose work – both ratting and rabbiting with them – for he believes that good ratting ferrets also make good rabbit-killing ferrets, and in those days you either used a liner, or sat outside a warren waiting for the fitch to return, neither of which was desirable; kills below ground were always dreaded in those days. Opinions differ greatly on this matter, but I have always used my ferrets for both rat-

ting and rabbiting, and have found them to be well suited to both roles. I do not believe, nor have I experienced, that a ratting ferret is any more prolific at killing rabbits. In fact, if a ratting ferret were to 'jib' at rat, that is, if it refused to work them any more after being bitten, then it could still have a secure future as a rabbit hunter.

Derek bred from those first few ferrets, and the line continues today. Jack Howarth's ferrets also went into the mix, and a little later two jills from the Abbot brothers were also brought into the strain. They were excellent workers, and Derek had years of service from these two ferrets.

Derek is now forty-five years of age and he continues to work, show and breed the same strain of ferret that he started all those years ago, though they now come in a variety of different colours, far more than in those early days. His daughter Katie is also very keen on ferrets, and he is hoping that she will take over and continue the strain when the time comes.

Ferreting rabbits is a very effective way of controlling these pests, but it is also a way of obtaining some of the healthiest meat available. Rabbit meat is full of vitamins and is lean, so it is good for both the heart and the figure. It is also a truly organic meat. Admittedly rabbits which feed in lowland pastures where chemicals are used may carry slight traces of these, but rabbits feeding on the untreated uplands make some of the most natural and healthy food available today. If it were not for the introduction and continuous outbreaks of myxomatosis, rabbiting would be a truly profitable venture.

CHAPTER 6

RABBITING WITH DOGS

Jake and Rocky, two excellent rabbiting dogs

I have been very fortunate over the years in that I have always managed to acquire good rabbiting dogs that have blossomed into excellent all-rounders with time and experience. Merle was probably my best, though Bess, an ex-track-racing greyhound, was also a superb hunter of coney. In my youth there were plenty of flapping tracks – that is, unlicensed greyhound racing stadiums where one could easily pick up a dog that had either just not made the grade as a racer, or was getting too old, maybe five years of age, and was being replaced by a younger dog. Bess was one of these. She had been raced for a few years and was now considered too old to compete, though she couldn't have been more than four or five when this decision was taken.

She then fell into the hands of Neville Mawson, who had the very suspect way of 'training' his running dogs mentioned earlier, and in no time at all was a nervous wreck. Nev had killed a few cats with her, but had found her useless for rabbiting or hare coursing on the big fields of Lincolnshire, punishing her for failing to catch, and so she was passed on to me, and became the first running dog I actually owned. I had, however, already hunted with quite a number by that time, which meant that I was not ignorant to the ways of lurchers and greyhounds (I had run a few ex-track-racing greyhounds before owning one), and I quickly set about putting her right. She had lost a lot of weight, and so the first thing to do was to provide her with a good balanced diet. A few days' rest would help, but after that she would have plenty of exercise, particularly roadwork, which would help build muscle and harden pads.

'Socializing' the Hunting Dog

I was obliged to 'break' her to cats, too, for my mother had three or four at the time and my life would not have been worth living had Bess killed any. Also, the farms where I hunted always had a cat or two around the place. I poached a lot in those days, it is true, but I also worked on a few farms, helping out at haymaking time and in the dairy and suchlike, and I had permission to hunt on these places, so it was essential that my dog did not go after cats. Ex-track-racing greyhounds are devils for cats, and even for small dogs such as Yorkshire terriers, and so it is really vital

that they are properly socialized as soon as possible. This can be done easily by 'breaking' them to cats, and also exercising them in public parks and places where they will frequently meet with other dogs of all shapes and sizes. Racing greyhounds do not lead social lives, and so this is essential for the hunting man.

I quickly set about socializing my bitch, and found that with Bess this was child's play, though some dogs do take much longer to train than others. Bess was so nervous and terrified of a beating that when she came into contact with our cats, it took only a firm command to 'leave' for her to realize that these creatures were to be left strictly alone from now on. I walked her every day in public parks, and she met other dogs without any problems whatsoever. Just a couple of weeks later she was completely broken to cats and all forms of farm livestock, was well socialized, and had put on weight and muscle. She was a fine specimen, and I felt she was now ready for her first outing.

A First Outing

On that day I went with Dec, Nev, Sam and Gordon, all members of the same poaching gang – though I couldn't help feeling that this was foolishness, because if Bess failed to perform, then I was in for a real showing up. Nev already thought nothing of her, but I was determined to prove that it was his methods, not the abilities of the dog, that were to blame for her previous failures – and I would have witnesses to prove it. We were hunting the high ground, and Laddie, Gordon's Bedlington/greyhound, had his nose to the ground and soon put up a hare. This was tricky ground, but still, Cassy, Laddie and

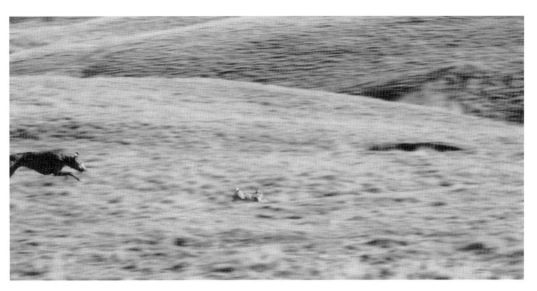

A lurcher giving chase.

Shandy gave chase eagerly. Shandy belonged to Nev and was another ex-track-racing greyhound from Ireland, in fact from the famous Westmead kennels, because she hadn't quite made the grade as a racing dog: very high standards were set at these kennels, and the failure rate was high. Shandy had nevertheless proved to be a useful hare dog in Lincolnshire, but here the heather and rock made the going difficult, and the three dogs gave chase in vain. I was across the valley and so thought it a waste of time to slip Bess, despite the fact that she was doing cartwheels on the end of her lead, keen as mustard to go. That hare soon made its escape and we moved on, now hunting the pastures by Whitewall Wood.

Laddie entered the wood and put his nose down, soon bushing a rabbit out into the open field where Shandy, Cassy and Bess were slipped. They had quite a bit of ground to make up and soon disappeared over the crest of a small hill in hot pursuit.

They must have quickly turned the rabbit, for it was soon running back towards us and the three dogs were close behind, Shandy just ahead of Cassy, with Bess in the rear. The rabbit was now making a straight run for the cover of trees and bushes ahead, but all the time the dogs were gaining, with Bess, to my delight, now coming through the middle of the other two dogs and inching ahead, slowly but surely. And then, only a few feet from certain escape, Bess just took the lead and struck, picking up her rabbit a split second before the other dogs made a grab for their quarry. It had been a very exciting run and a superb strike; accurate and incredibly quick, so quick that the rabbit hadn't time to turn, and Dec, Gordon and Sam congratulated me on the condition and abilities of my bitch.

Nev, however, was not pleased at all. He snatched up the rabbit and stuffed it inside his jacket, claiming that Shandy had caught it before any of the other dogs, despite the fact that all the others came to my defence, saying Bess was responsible and that I should rightly have the prize. Nev was having none of it, but I wasn't bothered. My bitch was now fit and healthy and she had proved her quality, and I could quite understand that he couldn't admit that *his* bitch had been beaten by the dog he had written off as useless, and had given away, only a couple of weeks ago. Besides, he had forgotten to empty the bladder of that rabbit, so I chuckled to think that he would soon be wet through (once the rabbit is dead and the muscles have had time to relax properly, you can empty the bladder by holding the rabbit up and squeezing the lower abdomen until all the urine has flowed out).

Bess never looked back after this, and enjoyed years of rabbit hunting; I also used her for foxes, rats and, of course, the odd hare course.

The Tale of the Missing Sunday Roast

Greyhounds are not known for their intelligence, but Bess achieved a misdemeanour which made me think they are not *that* daft, after all. In our household Sunday was traditionally a day of roast chicken with all the trimmings, and it was a day we all looked forward to with great eagerness indeed. As usual we were all out for the morning, after a night of hard frost; I had taken the dogs into the woods where the tree branches were covered in thousands of ice crystals, the surrounding fields white, the grass crisp and crunchy underfoot. Bess had chased a few rabbits around the woods, but they were close to their burrows and escaped easily. When I

got back home the delicious scent of roast chicken filled the house, but there was another couple of hours to wait before lunch, so we all got on with our different tasks. Then some time later I heard Mum shouting, 'Where's t'bloody chicken gone?'

When Mum shouted, we listened, as did our closest neighbours! Nearly jumping out of our seats at such an unexpected interruption of a peaceful Sunday afternoon, we ran into the kitchen in the hopes that Mum had been absent-minded again: we had known her put the milk in the oven and the salt and pepper in the fridge before now! But our hopes were dashed, for that chicken could not be found anywhere. Bess, alongside Butch, the family pet dog, was asleep in front of the fire – and she looked just a little too content for comfort, her belly undoubtedly distended as though she had just eaten something. Our suspicions were aroused, and we kept on throwing black looks at her – but we couldn't prove anything. We told Mum that she must have forgotten to put the chicken in the roasting tray, and Bess must have got on to the table and taken it. The trouble with this theory was that, not so long ago, the house had been full of the familiar smell of cooking chicken, though we wondered if that had been our imaginations misleading us, a sort of 'wishful thinking' effect.

My brother, Mike, and I decided to watch Mum carefully during the next Sunday lunch preparations, just to make sure that that chicken made it safely into the oven, for our minds were made up: Mum had 'gaffed' again, putting an empty baking tray in the oven and absent-mindedly leaving that chicken for Bess to steal. And that is exactly what we did: we saw that chicken secure in the oven, and then got on with our day, content in the knowledge that we would have a feast fit for a king in just a couple of hours or so. But then: 'What't bloody 'ell's goin' on?' Mum shouted from the kitchen. Mike and I stared at one another in horror: 'Oh no, it couldn't have happened again!', we were both thinking as we ran to the kitchen – but it had! But how? Bess again looked content and well fed, just as she had last week – but this time we had made certain that the chicken had gone into the oven! The tray was still there, and the unmistakable traces of chicken could be seen in the juices. It was a real mystery.

By the third week we were determined to enjoy our Sunday lunch complete with chicken, and so posted a guard to watch over that oven. Mum was to remain in the living room and carefully watch over the roasting chicken, just in case a tramp or somesuch was getting into our kitchen and stealing our roast; for though we suspected Bess, we felt this was unrealistic after the previous week, for how could she be to blame when we had seen the meat put safely inside the oven?

Mike and I were upstairs when we heard Mum shout, 'Bess, get off it!' but we were down those stairs and in the kitchen within a few seconds: there was Bess in sulky mood, receiving a severe ticking off while Mum rescued a rather dishevelled, but just about perfectly done, golden brown chicken, with just a few holes in it where Bess had obviously taken hold. Mum had been dozing in front of the fire when she felt the dog brush gently against her legs. She watched closely as Bess stealthily approached the cooker, her slinking movement betraying her duplicit intentions. Remarkably, she then hooked her nose under the handle of the oven door and pulled it open, about halfway. This door was on a spring action and would only

remain open if it was pulled right down, so there were only a few seconds to spare before the door would shut again. Mum was amazed at what she then witnessed, for Bess now moved very quickly and snatched the chicken, hot as it was, from the baking tray, and carried it across the room before putting it on the floor with the obvious intention of devouring every last scrap of it. The oven door meanwhile closed of its own accord. It was, in fact, the perfect crime. Mum, however, immediately putting a stop to the stolen meal, while severely reprimanding the criminal.

Nevertheless, all of us were amazed at her method, for up until that time I had not credited her with a great deal of intelligence. We are constantly told that greyhounds lack intelligence, but she is the only dog I know that had worked out how to get a chicken out of an oven! Not only was she a poacher's dog, but she began poaching off the poacher!

Dogs should never be given cooked bones, as these can splinter and cause fatal internal injury, so it is also remarkable that she escaped any serious health problems in the course of her illegal activity. Bess never attempted this again, though she did get up to other mischief. She was quite a character, but it was as a worker that she is best remembered.

Retrieving Live to Hand

I used Bess for lamping quite a bit, despite the fact that she was white and tan in colour: poachers usually use dark-coloured dogs so they cannot be seen whilst hunting at night, or whilst fleeing from keepers. I never even attempted to train her to retrieve, for I had been told that greyhounds simply wouldn't do this. However, I had always run her alongside another dog, usually Cassy, and few dogs will retrieve when worked in pairs, for they will jealously try to claim the prey for themselves. For this reason it is always best to run one dog at a time, because they are more likely to retrieve the rabbit; furthermore the meat will be less bruised, if at all. If the meat is intended only for the dogs themselves, then of course this doesn't matter, but if it is for human consumption, either at home or through a game dealer, then it is important to make certain that it isn't bruised in the slightest. In this situation a soft-mouthed dog is essential – that is, one that will not use a crushing bite and kill its prey. A dog that retrieves live to hand is essential for those who use the meat for themselves and their families, or sell it on to others.

On this particular night I was running Bess alone and we were lamping fields that we hunted on a fairly regular basis: lowland pastures that were used to graze a large herd of cattle belonging to the nearby dairy. This was winter and so the cows were in from the fields, leaving our hunting grounds free from disturbance. The night was dark and windy, the clouds rushing by overhead across a moonless sky: perfect conditions for the poacher. I swept the field with the beam and the bright eyes of a fox were picked up as it left the field and headed out on to the motorway embankment in the distance. I took the beam off it and swung it to the left, finally picking up a 'sitter'. Bess was loosed and off she went, running down the beam until her shadow leapt in front of her and made the rabbit run. Sometimes rabbits will sit tight, no matter what, when the beam shines, and I have known them stay put so they could be easily picked up, even by the poacher himself. Yet at other times they will run as soon as they realize they are in real danger.

Bess was after it like a shot. Greyhounds take a little time to move up into top gear, but it wasn't long before she rapidly closed on her quarry, striking, but

One dog will usually retrieve well.

over-running as her prey turned suddenly, tightly. She recovered soon after, and again began moving up into top gear, bearing down on the rabbit rapidly and turning it again. The rabbit now ran towards the edge of the field and headed out on to the pavement, running now out of sight under the motorway bridge alongside a quiet country lane which, thankfully, carried no traffic at this time of night.

Bess was in hot pursuit, and ignored my cries for her to return, for she was close to her quarry and could easily see it in the dim light from the street lamps. There is a small pasture on the other side of this bridge and the rabbit must have made it to this: but Bess was determined, and eventually put in a successful strike. I was most impressed when she came bounding along the pavement towards me, the rabbit in her mouth.

We returned to the pasture and began lamping again, picking up another bunny that had obviously been lamped before, for it ran the instant the beam settled on it. Bess was quite some way off, but her long bounds soon made up the ground and she was on it in no time. The rabbit was so hard pressed that, like the previous one, it too headed under the fence and out on to the pavement, going under the motorway bridge and making for the small pasture on the other side.

Bess was quickly through the fence and followed her quarry on to the pasture, where again, thanks to the street lamps illuminating the area, she caught her prey, carrying it back to me in the same manner. Those rabbits either headed towards that pasture out of desperation, or, more likely, they came from a warren situated there, making their way under that bridge every night in order to feed on the rich pastures on the other side.

The Working Dog 'Living In'

As already observed, greyhounds have a reputation for being of limited intelligence, and they are also said to be unbiddable. I believe this is true when they are reared in kennel and have contact with humans and other dogs for only limited periods of time, but when reared with the family, living indoors and socializing with humans and other animals throughout the day, then I believe their intelligence levels improve dramatically. Countrymen will often tell you – the older generation anyway – that you will spoil a dog and make it unfit for work if you keep it indoors and allow it the luxury of a warm fireside and company with adults and children alike, but this assumption is simply not true. Dogs in fact show more intelligence, and are far more biddable when they are reared indoors and have unlimited company with people and other animals such as cats and other dogs. To my mind, a dog is spoiled when it is locked up in a kennel for twenty-three hours a day and deprived of any contact with humans and other dogs.

Another theory is that dogs reared and living indoors will not cope well with bad weather. Again, I have found this theory to be absolutely unfounded. I have had a few kennel dogs, but the majority have 'lived in', and my dogs work from late August through to the latter half of March, year in, year out, in often atrocious conditions (I am no 'fair weather hunter'), and although they do sometimes look uncomfortable, in the same way that I do when the weather is bad, they have no problems coping with it. In fact, as soon as they get a scent, or a run, they quickly forget about the cold or wet conditions. All our dogs

Large catches can be made on the lamp. (Clifford Yates with his lurcher.)

living indoors with the family have proved to be hardy, easily trained and superb workers. The more socialized a dog is, the more easily trained it will be, and the better worker it will make: this I can absolutely guarantee.

Obedience in the Lamping Dog

The lamping dog must be fleet of foot and have some measure of intelligence, for it must quickly learn to spot 'sitters' in a beam, and then run in and pick them up. This will come with experience, though it helps if the apprentice can watch an experienced dog in action a few times before starting itself.

The lamping lurcher must also be obedient. If a rabbit jumps a wall, or gets through a fence, or runs over a hill out of sight, then the lurcher must learn to come off its quarry as soon as the beam is shut off and its master calls. This is essential. Firstly, poachers need a lurcher to return immediately, in order to escape the attentions of keepers or farmers. Of course, I

encourage all hunters to seek permission on any land they hunt, and those who poach must be prepared to face the consequences of their actions; but when I was a lad and did quite a lot of poaching, a dog returning on command was very important, for quick getaways were essential on more than one occasion!

Secondly, poachers are very often not familiar with the land they hunt, as they will not have been able to walk over it during daylight hours and see possible danger areas that can be avoided whilst lamping. In this situation, if a dog should jump a wall or a fence, or run over a hill in the pitch black of night, it risks serious injury, and even death. I know of stone walls along the top of quarry faces and natural crags, and a dog jumping such obstacles could easily fall to its death. Hence the reason why a lurcher must immediately cease giving chase when the beam is switched off and the master calls. If a lurcher were to prove disobedient, then lamping such fields bordered by quarries and suchlike, would be unwise indeed. However, if it does cease running as soon as the beam is off and the command is given, then such places are accessible to the hunter.

Railways cut through fields, and the pastures alongside them are very often extremely rich hunting grounds. But again, if a lurcher were disobedient and got its nose to the ground once the beam was off, ignoring its master's cries to return, then it would be at risk of getting on to the tracks, where it would obviously be in severe danger. Rabbits live on these embankments and will usually make for them, and a well-trained lurcher will catch many on this type of ground (though it must be avoided for those who have less biddable dogs).

Coping with Accidents

The advantage of having permission for either ferreting, or lamping, or simply day-time running on rabbits, is that you can walk over the ground before hunting it, and all high risk areas can be noted and, if needs be, avoided. However, no matter how careful you are, accidents can happen – though when you consider the number of times a dog is hunted, these are usually quite rare. Bess had two major accidents during her long and prolific career, and there was nothing I could have done to avoid them.

The first occurred when a friend and I were hunting around an abandoned farm where rabbits were found in abundance. They lived in drains, piles of tumbled-down stone, and just about anywhere else they could manage to crawl inside, even in the cellars of the old farmhouse. Carl had a lurcher, Major, a cross between a labrador and a whippet, and he was a good hunter, though he was quite heavily built, as you would expect from such a cross, and was just a little too slow to make a good catch dog. Merle, my lurcher, was heavily built

too, being a mixture of greyhound, whippet, bull terrier and either beagle or foxhound blood; but again, he was a superb hunter, and caught far more rabbits than Major. By comparison, it was good to have Bess there, for the faster chases.

Rabbits were usually found skulking all over this place and so ferreting was very often unnecessary. Major and Merle would get their noses to the ground and it wasn't long before a rabbit, and very often a few of them, would be flushed from some hiding place among the debris scattered around. Merle put a rabbit up from out of a small pile of stones and Bess was quickly on it. When lurchers work together, they quickly learn to operate as a close unit and will read each other well. Bess had come to know when Merle was close to flushing his quarry, and she often correctly read the way in which the quarry would run. This she did with this particular rabbit, and she was close on its heels in no time at all. It ran on to the farm track, however, and went under a closed gate. By the time Bess saw the obstacle looming just ahead, it was too late: she put the brakes on immediately, but slid on the loose gravel, hitting the gate at high speed and with a sickening thud. She howled in agony and could barely walk when I reached her. The first thing to do was to get her to the vet (my vet at that time was Peter Nut – his brass plate read 'P. Nut' – and his wife, believe it or not, was called Hazel), though I had a few miles to walk to get there, and believe me, a 26in greyhound becomes very heavy when carrying it for that distance.

Bess was treated and soon healed, but the emotional scars were only too evident during her first outing after her accident and recovery. We were out lamping and rabbits were bounding all over the place. I singled one out in the beam and slipped her, but she simply ignored it and would not budge: the accident had completely destroyed her confidence, and even during daylight hours, she would not run. I had no idea what to do about this predicament – until I spoke to the local ice-cream van driver.

Phil had at one time been heavily involved in racing greyhounds, but he and his two brothers also enjoyed a spot of rabbiting and hare coursing. Phil told me to take my bitch out with another dog, both during the day and on the lamp at night, and allow her to watch another dog at work. No matter how keen she was, I must not slip her. This I had to do for a few occasions, before trying her once more.

Dec Feeney ran Cassy during these outings, and it wasn't long before Bess was doing cartwheels on the end of her lead, though I fought the impulse to slip her; she became more and more frustrated, in the end chewing at the leather slip, she was so desperate to work. Once the excitement and frustration had reached its peak, I began working her again and in no time at all she was back to her old self. This method certainly worked, and is one I can definitely recommend to anyone who has a running dog that refuses to give chase after an accident has destroyed its confidence.

The second accident occurred when I was out hawking with a friend who owned a buzzard. Buzzards are not the ideal falconer's bird, but some do make quite competent rabbiting hawks. This one, Storm, was owned by the young Melvyn Westwood, who was quite a character. Melvyn was scientifically minded and had made a name for himself after learning how to make home-made bombs. He had been forced to curtail his activities, however, after testing one device inside his dad's garden shed and blowing it to pieces!

Storm had been taken from the wild while still in the nest, and his training had begun once the feathers were strong enough to cope. Buzzards eat quite a bit of carrion in the wild, hence the reason for their reputation as lazy hunters, but they will take live rabbits expertly when they are hungry enough, and so Melvyn found his bird to be useful out in the hunting field.

We had gone to a large warren that always held, every time we visited; to get to it we had to climb a steep bank and then negotiate a sheep-wire fence, with barbed wire running along the top throughout its length. But because of the steep bank leading up to this, it was an awkward spot to get over. Bess, knowing of the large rabbit population inhabiting this place, was obviously excited and went on ahead, and attempted to jump the fence. I usually lifted her over, but this time she didn't give me the chance.

Greyhounds can jump quite well, but from where she took off she never stood any chance of clearing the fence. She got her front end over well enough, but then she came crashing down on the barbed wire, which stuck into her hip joints and hung her by the back legs, the cruel wire tearing into her flesh and becoming quite deeply embedded. She howled in pain and I attempted to lift her off the fence, but from where I was standing I couldn't do it. Bess was the most placid dog in the world, but still she bit my hand, confused with agony and panic. Melvyn, with Storm on his gloved fist, was unable to help, so I scrambled over the fence and, after quite a struggle, managed to free her at last. She was torn quite badly, but at least the more vulnerable underbelly had been spared damage. If the wire had pierced here, instead of at the hip joint, then things would have been far worse.

These two accidents certainly gave us all a fright, but when you consider the hundreds of times over several seasons that Bess was run, to have only two serious mishaps in all that time just goes to show how seldom this sort of thing happens.

Training the Lamping Dog

The lamping dog must be well trained, returning to its master once the beam is switched off, or on command. A dark colour is essential for poachers, though not so crucial on permission land. Some will say that light-coloured dogs are more easily seen by prey, but I have never found there to be any difference in a night's takings whether using dark- or light-coloured lurchers, and I have hunted many times with both types. What is important is that they are silent, because those that bark are likely to disturb other rabbits feeding in and around the field that is being hunted. And poachers would certainly be detected if their lurchers went barking around every field hunted, in their pursuit of illegal game! Melvyn Westwood had a lurcher that used to bark while giving chase (a fault blamed on early entering, but more likely because there was either hound or terrier somewhere in its make-up), and he had some alarming experiences with farmers alerted by the noise as the dog chased around their fields. One farmer, 'Rickets' by name, was well known for putting bacon rind and salt in his shotgun: fired at fairly close range, this put a 'sting in the tail' of his pellets, causing his victims to flee holding their backside! Mel never actually admitted that he was one of these 'victims', but he never put up a spirited defence either, so I suspect there was at least some truth in it.

The most effective way of taking rabbits on the lamp is to concentrate on 'sitters'. Once one is in the beam, try to get as close as possible in order that your youngster can pinpoint the rabbit, either by scent or, more especially, by sight. With time and experience a young dog will soon learn how to pick up tight-sitting rabbits, though they will learn much more quickly by watching an experienced dog in action.

A lurcher is best entered to rabbits on the lamp once it has a couple of months of experience during the daytime, and you can do no better than to start a dog whilst out ferreting, and then allow it to progress to the lamp. This allows the dog to become very familiar with its quarry, enabling it to use both sight and scent in its work, and it also gives it time to develop into a competent catch dog, long before lamping begins. It is no good starting a dog on the lamp when it has no previous experience of hunting coney, for it would surely miss several, and you would run the risk of making most of the rabbits in that area lamp-shy within a very short space of time. A dog that has previous experience of ferreting and day-time catching will learn far more quickly when you start to take it lamping with you. I must point out here that lamp-shy rabbits are a huge nuisance! As soon as the lamp goes on, they run for the hedge or their burrow somewhere nearby, leaving you sweeping an empty field with the beam.

Once a few sitting rabbits have been caught, the next step is to allow a youngster to run. Bigger fields are best for starting a novice, for if a rabbit does run, then there is plenty of room in which the dog can work. Easy runs are essential at this stage, because hard runs, or short, unsuccessful runs that end with the rabbit either disappearing underground or through a hedge, will very quickly destroy confidence, especially in the more timid breeds.

Which Cross Makes the Best Rabbiting Dog?

Lurchers with terrier blood such as Bedlington will have more determination than will something like a whippet/greyhound, and will be far less phased by unsuccessful runs. The only trouble with terrier crosses is that they can yap when giving chase, and they are usually hard-mouthed, too – that is, they will kill the rabbit and bruise the meat. Nevertheless they make formidable rabbiting dogs, and crosses with such blood, such as the Bedlington/whippet, take some beating.

The retrieve. A Bedlington/whippet lurcher. (Shane Southern)

I have found that the labrador, or retriever cross, is very useful at both day and night rabbiting. They have excellent noses, are biddable, soft-mouthed, will naturally retrieve prey, and are usually silent at work. The only drawback is that they are often a little too heavy for the quick bursts of speed and sharp turns that are required in a rabbiting dog. If you want this type, then the whippet/retriever cross whippet, rather than the first cross, is by far the best option, for these are much lighter in build and retain the speed and agility of the whippet.

The Bedlington/whippet first cross is very useful indeed, but put back to a whippet, the second cross will be even more useful. At the time of writing there is much talk of which cross makes the best rabbiting dog. Opinions, as with all subjects, differ considerably, and some suggest the collie/greyhound is by far the best, while others go for the Bedlington/greyhound, and quite a number are adamant that the pure whippet knocks spots off the pair of these. My own humble opinion is that you cannot beat the whippet/Bedlington second cross to a whippet. Whippets are fast and agile, but they are neither hardy enough to stand up to severe winter weather, the time when rabbiting is in full swing, nor determined enough to make the very best rabbit hunters. Bedlington blood produces both hardiness and determination. True, the first cross may be inclined to yap when giving chase, for terrier blood can produce this effect, but the second cross will rarely bark and they are much softer in the mouth. Some Bedlingtons, however, are mute even when up to a fox (a result of bull terrier blood being added to the mix probably during the nineteenth century) and so yapping does not occur, though this fault can crop up in some Bedlington crosses.

Whippets are very often run with jackets on during the winter months, and I find this totally unacceptable in a dog required to work for me: this is because jackets could easily catch on fences and other obstacles while the dog is giving chase, and thus could cause injury. A touch of Bedlington blood will make the use of jackets totally unnecessary. A chap in Ramsbottom in Lancashire bred a strain of whippet/Bedlington for decades, and they were superb rabbiting dogs, ideal for ferreting and bushing, and very useful on the lamp too, especially for taking 'sitters', or those rabbits that suddenly leap up and run, just as the dog is about to strike. The whippet blood means that this cross is incredibly quick off the mark, and the Bedlington blood provides the courage and determination, as well as the stamina, to run hard throughout the day or night and to strike with deadly force.

For hare coursing, give me a lurcher with quite a bit of greyhound blood every time. For rabbiting, however, a lurcher with whippet blood, rather than a pure whippet, or a greyhound-based lurcher, is, in my opinion, unbeatable. Greyhound blood usually produces size and it can take a while for such a lurcher to get into its stride. Whippet blood will mean that a lurcher is on the smaller side and will have that sharp burst of speed, along with great agility, that I prefer in a rabbiting dog. Cassy, Dec's lurcher, was a whippet/greyhound and she was very useful indeed, both for rabbits and hares; however, she wasn't the cleverest dog I have come across. Dec wasn't too bothered though, for she caught him plenty of game for the pot, and would take anything he encouraged, from cats to chickens. I always thought he was an idiot allowing his bitch to kill cats, for those claws can easily take out the eye of a running dog, and most rely on sight for success. Killing cats can so easily cost you good permission, too.

Training the Young Lurcher

A young lurcher will be ready to start on rabbits by the time it is eight months or so. Before this time the dog is developing rapidly, and work – or too much of it, anyway – could cause damage to muscle tissue, which may result in problems later in life.

I have started dogs at just six months when I was young and inexperienced, but I would not do so nowadays because at that age they are not fully developed. By eight months, development has slowed down quite a bit, and muscle and bone will be better able to cope with work. However, even at this age, some lurchers are not mentally mature enough and can be easily

I prefer to start a dog in the day time.

put off. If in doubt, wait until ten, or even twelve months, before starting a puppy. There are no set rules in this situation, for individual dogs have different needs.

As I have said, I personally prefer to start a novice on daytime rabbits, but many others prefer to enter on the lamp, because they feel they can get close to the quarry and thus give the dog a better chance of a successful run. This method does have serious drawbacks, however, such as creating lamp-shy rabbits, for young lurchers will usually miss several before making a successful strike. Furthermore, many rabbits will sit tight during the daytime, and you can get close enough to give your dog a better chance – though even then, quite a number may be missed. In this situation, do not be tempted to net a rabbit and release it on to a large field for your dog to chase, because you would run the risk of prosecution for cruelty – and might also risk putting rabbiting on the 'banned' list. Always strive to kill quickly and cleanly. Be persistent, and eventually your dog will make a successful catch.

Starting a Puppy

Use common sense when starting a puppy. For instance, do not slip it at rabbits feeding close to hedgerows, fences or warrens, but look for a squatter out in the middle of a field. These are sure to be encountered at some time or other, especially during the early morning or evening, when rabbits will feed more boldly. Ferreting rabbits is a very effective way of carrying out control, and the rabbiting dog is absolutely essential for this activity. Apprentice lurchers, or maybe terriers if that is your preference, will quickly learn how to mark warrens as occupied, or otherwise, and a great deal of time and effort may be saved by such dogs: without a 'true' marker, you could spend an age netting and ferreting unoccupied warrens (though some ferrets will not enter empty burrows). With a faithful lurcher or terrier by your side, only occupied warrens will be worked, which means that you are operating at 100 per cent efficiency, and your pest control will keep the landowner happy. I would not be without a good marking dog, and

Lurchers on guard lest a rabbit bolts.

Rocky watches for bolting rabbits.

this ability usually comes with experience, though some mark true from day one.

A young dog is best worked on the slip whilst walking up to daytime rabbits, ferreting, or lamping, until a suitable measure of obedience is achieved. Once some experience has been gained, it will be possible, even advisable, to leave your lurcher free. This has certain benefits. When rabbits hit the net, for instance, it is best to teach your dog to leave well alone, but the lurcher should be encouraged to remain by the netted quarry until it is safely dealt with, lest it get out of the net. When a rabbit is loose, a lurcher will soon learn to quickly snap it up before it gets into its stride. This is also true of rabbits that bolt from unnetted holes.

While loose, a lurcher, through sound, scent and vibrations undetected by the human hunter, will often be able to follow the rabbit's progress underground, much as a pack of fellhounds can follow the progress of fox and terrier inside a deep borran earth, and will know which hole the rabbit is going to bolt from. Thus it can often snap up the fleeing quarry very quickly indeed. Merle, my lurcher, became very adept at snaffling bolting rabbits before they had cleared a couple of yards.

A young dog is best worked on the slip.

At one spot, a three-holed burrow on the side of a steep wooded ghyll, a place we were unable to net for one reason or another, Merle was placed close to the warren while the ferret was entered. Whilst the ferret is working, it is important to be silent, not only to allow the rabbits to flee undisturbed from the fitch, but also to give the dog a chance to fathom exactly what is going on in the darkness below. We watched as Merle paced quietly about this difficult burrow, and then went suddenly into action, speedily snatching up a bolting rabbit before it knew what was going on. He retrieved his prize and went back to his station, doing exactly the same thing with the second and final rabbit. Without a decent dog, that place would have been best left.

The Terrier as a Rabbiting Dog

Terriers also make superb rabbiting dogs. Lurchers on the smaller side, in my opinion, are the most useful, and a height of

Terriers also make superb rabbiting dogs. (Flint, bred out of Fell and Mist and owned and worked by Carl Noon.)

Alfie, owned and worked by Neil Wilson and bred out of Fell and Mist. A good sort!

Terriers at work. (a)

(b) Entering a rabbit run.

(c) On the scent.

(d) Waiting for the bolt.

(e) Giving chase.

(f) Chasing coney through undergrowth.

around 18 to 20in is ideal, for such dogs are extremely quick off the mark and are small enough to 'bush' rabbits from most places. I would not rule out larger running dogs, however, for I have run quite a number up to 26in, and have found them useful, though not quite as effective as the smaller, more nimble dogs, especially at snatching up bolting rabbits.

A combination of terrier and lurcher is lethal. Terriers are determined workers and will find and flush rabbits from the densest undergrowth, ignoring tight passages laden with thorns, which scratch ears and heads quite badly. I have seen lurchers refuse to enter certain coverts, especially dense brambles, but terriers are game for anything and no rabbit can escape their attentions.

Terriers also make great marking dogs and they too will learn to snatch up rabbits bolting close by, though they are stubborn and headstrong enough to make training much more difficult, especially

when attempting to teach them to leave a netted rabbit well alone! When working terriers and lurchers together, the team will soon learn to read exactly what is going on and what is required in certain situations, quickly becoming very effective at working as a unit so that quite a number of conies are caught. One terrier and one lurcher can be a devastating combination when bushing and ferreting rabbits. However, jealousy can fester when two or more dogs work together, and an otherwise soft-mouthed dog can easily take to killing rabbits, rather than retrieving them live to hand, when they fear that the other dog will claim the prize.

There are benefits and drawbacks to working two or more dogs together. If you are not selling any of the catch to a game dealer and the rabbits will only be used as ferret and dog food, then a hard-mouthed dog isn't necessarily a drawback; but if the meat is for human consumption, then a soft-mouthed dog is essential, and you would be far better off working just the one dog.

Starting with a puppy is always the best policy, and teaching it to come on command and to retrieve is essential, as well as breaking to ferrets and livestock. Firmly telling your dog to 'leave' when showing it a ferret and farm livestock is a simple way of demonstrating that they are to be left strictly alone, but along with this you must make certain that your lurcher, or terrier, or perhaps both, are very familiar with these animals and come to accept them fully, with no hint of an interest in attacking them. When breaking to ferret, make sure the fitch does not bite the dog, for this could result in tension building, or even retaliation, and the breaking process could then be seriously hindered.

The Return and the Retrieve

Getting a puppy to return on command is simple: just give your new pup a name and stick with it, so that it quickly knows you are calling it; changing names only confuses a puppy, so pick one carefully and then stick with it. The response may be slow at first, so I use dog chocolates as a reward for obedience to this command; a pup will soon come on call, knowing it will be rewarded.

The retrieve, however, should not be rewarded with treats. For one thing, a rabbit will be far more interesting than a dog chocolate and the swap will not entice a puppy. Using an old teddy, or something similar (preferably a piece of rabbit fur), simply throw the object and then call the dog to you, rewarding with praise once your pup has released its prize and allowed you to take it. The release can be encouraged by firmly telling it to 'drop'. If

you use chocolates on the retrieve, the pup is likely to drop the dummy as it returns, so the lesson will not be learnt. Make these training sessions fun and light-hearted, and reward with much praise, and the results should be satisfactory, if not amazing.

Some lurchers do not take to retrieving too well, but do not despair. I have seen lurchers retrieve dummies slowly and without enthusiasm, but they have brought rabbits to hand eagerly when out hunting. Merle was one of these. He hated retrieve training, despite my attempts to make the sessions fun, but still, he would retrieve rabbits eagerly, even when other dogs were around. Bess was another. In fact, she wouldn't retrieve dummies at all, yet she would retrieve while out in the hunting field. This is especially so when one dog is worked alone. As I have already stated, many will not retrieve while other dogs are around.

Once a rabbit is safely in a purse net, a lurcher must learn to leave well alone. This is a lesson quickly learnt by commanding your pup to 'drop', if it gets hold of the rabbit – but do not scold him: the last thing you want is to knock the confidence of your apprentice. After a few outings, the young entry will be chasing rabbits to ground, bushing them from undergrowth and reedbeds, marking warrens and standing on guard lest any escape the nets, or bolt from undetected holes which have not been netted. The dog will be fully broken to ferrets and farm livestock, and is coming on command.

I believe that now is the time to start lamping, for by this time your dog has a good measure of obedience, and knows what life is all about.

Chasing rabbits to ground.

Lurchers must learn to leave 'secured' rabbits. (a)

Tempted, but steady! (b)

Lamping

Good lamping kits can be obtained from suppliers listed in this book, and these should be fully charged before each use. All one has to do then is to wait for a moonless night with a bit of a wind whipping up; inform the farmer of your imminent visit so that he doesn't telephone the police thinking poachers are on his land; and then take the dog along where it will soon learn how to take night-time rabbits. Choose the 'sitters' to begin with, and walk as close to them as possible. Do not be surprised, however, if your youngster still misses, for I have seen many experienced dogs move in right on top of a squatting coney and still miss it. When slipping at runners, choose larger fields and make certain the dog has a realistic chance of making a catch. By flicking the beam off and calling to your dog, you will ensure a quick return, something that will guard against injuries, or even death, which sometimes occur when dogs jump fences or stone walls. Be observant, and if danger is lurking in the shadows, switch off the beam immediately and call your dog to return. Taking risks usually ends in tragedy while out lamping.

Conditioning the Rabbiting Dog

Conditioning the rabbiting dog is important. Warm, dry housing is essential, and good food is very important, though I have never used these so-called 'science diets' which, in my experience, are totally unnecessary. The competitive hare courser may use such diets to get the best out of his dogs, but the rabbit hunter has no need of such expensive foods. You may wish to use a complete food, though you can do no better than to feed your dog, terrier, lurcher, greyhound, whatever type you choose, on rabbit meat. When this is not available, simple tinned meat, or brawn, will suffice, along with a mixer biscuit. Rabbits can be boiled until the meat simply falls off the bone. The bones and the juices left can then be made into a vegetable broth which goes over the meat and biscuits, though the bones must be removed, every last one of them, before serving, for cooked bones of any sort are deadly to dogs and can easily tear the intestines. After hunting, I always give a little extra food for a day or two, for much weight will be lost during an average day.

Exercise is very important on non-hunting days, as this helps keep the dog fit enough for the rigours of the hunting field. During the summer off-season, one can afford to be a little slack with regard to exercise, but just before and during the season, peak fitness is essential. About a month before hunting will begin, start taking your rabbiting dog on longer walks and include roadwork, for this builds muscles and hardens the pads. Dogs running over thorn-covered ground and rocky landscapes will need toughened pads, so be diligent when conditioning your dog for work. A walk of an hour a day is ideal, though one must be realistic. Few can afford that amount of time due to work and family commitments, so a walk of half an hour should suffice, provided there is quite a bit of road walking included in that time. Two walks per day of half an hour each is the ideal, but few can spare that amount of time. The day after hunting, rest your dog completely and it should be ready to go again in next to no time.

At one time I would lamp for much of the night and then carry on catching rabbits during the early morning when many are found feeding far from home. This was especially the case when I poached alongside Declan Feeney, for he had a market for his rabbits and so aimed to catch as many as he could, thus early mornings were not wasted. By the time dawn came, we would be far from home, but still, heading back by a different route from the fields we had been lamping, we would spend quite a bit of time slipping our lurchers at feeding rabbits and adding quite a few more to our tally.

I would not recommend this, however, for it is a punishing schedule and will greatly reduce the working life of your lurcher. By providing at least one rest day between hunting forays, you will allow the muscles to recover and your dog will last for years to come; allow two days, or even three, and you preserve the working ability yet more. The more a dog is hunted, the less time it will last, and never take your dog out night after night, for the muscle and joint damage will mean that a dog will be burnt out in no time at all. It is not too much to expect seven or eight good seasons from a well-cared for lurcher, and some will go on for even longer. True, they will begin to slow down during their fifth or sixth season, but they will still be very useful as ferreting and lamping dogs in particular, for 'sitters' are easily picked up by an experienced dog. Overwork your lurcher, though, and you will probably be forced to retire it by the age of five or six, and, in some extreme cases, even younger.

A lurcher that is well housed, fed, exercised and rested, in some cases will still be useful at the age of nine and ten years. To some extent this will depend on the breeding of the dog: for example, greyhound-based lurchers, if they have quite a bit of this sighthound blood in their make-up, will age more quickly than one with quite

A keen marking dog (Jack, Tim Green's Plummer terrier).

Two ferreted rabbits.

a bit of collie, or Bedlington, in its bloodlines.

For the ferreting man, a marking dog is invaluable. Both terriers and lurchers make great marking dogs, and each individual will have its own way of letting its owner know that the warren is occupied. Some will dig at the entrance and pull huge chunks of turf away. Some will stand still while looking intently into the hole. Some will paw the entrance, while others will whine, standing immobile with one paw off the ground. It will take only a short time for you to know when your dog is marking. I do not encourage a dog to mark, nor do I reward it, this is just something they do naturally, in their own good time. Encouragement and rewards can lead to false marking, so allow the dog to mark in its own time, without any help, for they are quite capable of carrying out this feat without any assistance whatsoever. The bolting rabbit is the only reward they look for when marking!

Starting with a puppy is always the best policy, for few unspoilt rabbiting dogs will be offered for sale. This makes sense when one considers the amount of work that goes into training and developing a top class rabbit dog. A lurcher that acquits itself well during daytime runs and ferreting, as well as on the lamp, is worth its weight in gold, and few people with any sense would even consider parting with such a valuable, even priceless, animal. Buying a puppy from a reputable breeder of good working stock is by far the best policy for those who wish to have a first class rabbiting companion.

CHAPTER 7

THE PLUMMER
STRAIN ON UIST

I was out rabbiting with Tim Green of North Uist, and the winds raged constantly across the flat grasslands of our hunting grounds on South Uist – barren, treeless, stark, the green pastures of the crofts standing out against the clear blue of a winter sky. Merab, Tim's lurcher from Brian Plummer's old strain, had already nailed a rabbit that had sat tight and then raced for home at the very last minute. A few other rabbits had entered their warren as we pulled up, and Tim now began netting up in readiness to enter a ferret. He had two albinos with him that day, again, like the lurcher, from Plummer's old strain that can be traced right back to the fifties. A hob and a jill were to be used.

In the old days, most hobs were huge since generally they were liners, but nowadays a smaller hob is desirable, for rabbits can bolt past them more easily. The hobs of old would fill a tunnel completely, and thus many rabbits could not bolt, making kills inevitable. Jack, a Plummer terrier and a

Merab about to catch her rabbit as it heads for the warren.

Tim Green netting the holes. (a)

Thoroughly covering the holes. (b)

superb worker, had come along too. As we worked, netting up this huge warren, the wind made the going extremely difficult indeed, not only because it made our fingers numb and almost unworkable within seconds, but also because the nets were being blown every which way, making the setting of them near impossible. Some nets just wouldn't stay put, so they were rendered pretty useless, despite the fact that we attempted to reset them time and time again.

In most places the wind rages and then abates, if only for a few seconds, but in the Hebrides, especially along the flatlands which take the full force of the icy blast coming directly off the Atlantic, there is nothing to hinder their progress and so there was no let-up. My wife and I were staying in a caravan, and the wind simply sucked all the heat from our fire straight up the chimney, making the place about as warm as a fridge! We sat there with the walls of the caravan moving in and out due to the force of the gales, while we moved with them. We were there in February, a time when bad weather is most likely, and I asked Tim if the forecast had said when the wind would drop. 'Oh, aye,' he replied 'about August time, ah think they said!' I have never experienced winds like them before my trip to this part of the world, and it still chilled me to the bone, despite the layers I had on.

Tim wanted to take as many rabbits as possible from this area, for it was overrun with them, in order to keep the crofters happy; so we were ferreting for a while and then, once darkness had set in, were going to do some lamping.

The two ferrets were entered in different locations, and it wasn't long before rabbits began bolting. The nets failed miserably, due, of course, to the wind, but at least Merab was there. It wasn't long before she caught another rabbit as it headed for another hole to the warren. The going was very difficult, however, for quite a number simply popped out of one hole and then slipped into another nearby,

Apart from this one, the nets failed miserably due to the wind.

Plummer's strain of ferret. The hob and jill used that day.

giving the lurcher absolutely no chance of catching them. The rabbits were unwilling to run, and kept on dodging the ferrets and the lurcher, giving them the run around and escaping the nets that were being blown all over the place. With the nets now out of action completely and the lurcher having missed a few through no fault of her own, it was inevitable, I suppose, that the ferrets eventually made kills below. Tim had not bothered with a locator, for these warrens are shallow and, anyway, Jack would soon tell us where the ferrets had laid up.

He wandered around, testing the different entrances, and soon disappeared below ground. He dug on a little, but quickly reached his rabbit, pulling it clear of the warren with the ferret still attached. An old countryman I knew would do his ferreting in this way, and if a fitch made a kill, his long, slender, old-fashioned Jack Russell would locate rabbits in the same way. Jack marked another spot and the rabbit and ferret were out in no time. This marked the end of our ferreting, for the wind made netting up almost impossible and totally inef-

fective anyway, and the rabbits were just not willing to run for some reason, possibly the severe conditions; so it was decided to wait for darkness to set in and then begin lamping.

We headed to a nearby hostelry where drinks and food were enjoyed, in keen anticipation of the hunting ahead. Once darkness had swamped the last of the daylight, we set off to a patch Tim had saved especially for my visit: more flatlands adjoining a croft where the owner had asked Tim to reduce rabbit numbers, as they had swollen considerably of late. We were once again close to the sea, on flat, low-lying fields full of rich grasses, which attracted large numbers of coney. Where food is plentiful, rabbits breed at an even greater prolific rate, so it is important to keep on top of their numbers. These fields were ideal for lamping, being flat and large, and no doubt Tim uses such places when bringing on a youngster. The crop-growing season was just ahead, so he would be spending quite a bit of time here over the next few weeks, drastically reducing the population before the onset of spring and summer.

Merab waiting for a bolt.

A rabbit taken by Merab. Once dead, squeeze the urine from the bladder in this way.

Jack was leashed and I held him by my side, while Tim lamped the fields with Merab loose by his side. The powerful beam swept across the green flatlands and picked out hordes of coney, some running, others squatting stubbornly, foolishly. Merab was sent on, and she kept her gaze fixed on her quarry until she ran in and picked it up expertly. On occasion, she couldn't quite see her quarry and passed over it, but once running, was quickly into action, closing the gap between hunter and hunted rapidly, and striking with deadly accuracy. She had proved herself very useful as a ferreting and daytime-catch dog, but, I can assure you, she is red hot on the lamp, picking up rabbit after rabbit in double-quick time. It was like watching a conveyor belt of rabbits coming to Tim's hand!

The evening now took on a surreal quality, for believe it or not, Jack, a Plummer terrier, now replaced Merab while she rested awhile, leashed by my side. He was loose in the same manner and remained close to Tim's side while he lamped and picked up 'sitters'. He was then sent on and ran down the beam in exactly the same manner as the lurcher, striking once

he had spotted his rabbit. He was much harder-mouthed however, so the rabbits were dead on arrival, but that didn't really matter as these rabbits would be used to feed Tim and Sue's menagerie of wildcats, eagle owls, terriers, lurchers and ferrets, and any other beasts which could be found on their premises! Jack retrieved well for a terrier, especially when one considers that another dog was present, for terriers are the most jealous of dogs. He missed one or two and would go off baying into the night as he gave chase enthusiastically. Once the beam was off, however, he would soon be back by Tim's side, awaiting the presence of another squatting coney.

Another rabbit was just missed, for it sprang into action just before he could reach his prey and ran for the fence. However, he turned it several times and finally caught his rabbit as it attempted to get under the fence, which would have seen it safely through to the sand dunes beyond. A couple more were caught by Jack before Merab took over once more and added another few to the tally. If I hadn't have seen this for myself, I would have had difficulty believing that a terrier could be so useful on the lamp. Tim works

Merab continues to wait for the bolt . . .

. . . and secures her quarry.

A ferret sheltering from that awful wind.

most of his terriers in this way and often lamps with them in a pack. Well over thirty rabbits were accounted for that day, and both Jack and Merab played a very important part in the day's proceedings, not to mention the two ferrets. I had a great time on Uist and enjoyed working with the Plummer strain of ferret and lurcher, which have proved very useful indeed. The Plummer terriers, too, were exceptionally keen, and they eagerly flushed, chased and hunted their quarry.

Tim, Merab, Jack and a few rabbits taken that day.

CHAPTER 8

SHOOTING RABBITS

The control of rabbits by shooting can be very effective, and is best done with either ferrets, or decent bushing dogs, or preferably both. I have done plenty of ferreting for shooting men over the years, and my terriers have flushed several from undergrowth. I have also used lurchers in conjunction with the gun, but this can be a very risky business indeed. Those with guns must be alert at all times, and especially when lurchers are around, because they could easily take a shot at a rabbit that was being chased by the dog and both could be hit, even killed, if proper care wasn't taken. Of course, a shooter must be alert at all times, whether dogs are around or not, for farm animals and other hunting companions are also at risk – but this is especially true when lurchers are running loose.

I much prefer to use terriers for flushing rabbits to guns, and the best for this job are Jack Russells, simply because they are white, and thus more easily seen – though borders, fells, Bedlingtons or Patterdales will all do this job perfectly well. Teckels – that is, long-haired dachshunds – also make superb bushing dogs, but again, they are dark in colour and so are not so easily seen as white-bodied terriers. I have used both Russells and fells for flushing rabbits to guns, and with considerable success, but am far more comfortable when a light-coloured dog is working in this situation.

Shotgun Safety

Shotgun safety must be paramount in the mind of the rabbit hunter, and I strongly advise all who shoot to join the BASC (British Association for Shooting and Conservation) and to purchase their excellent *Handbook of Shooting*. The chapter on shotgun safety is invaluable, and all who shoot should be very familiar with this superb publication *before* even considering the use of guns. Common sense will dictate much of the safety procedures, such as treating every gun as though it were loaded, and taking precautions as a result. Carrying guns with the breach open is essential. Equally it is vital never to point a gun at anything but your intended target. When crossing rough ground and when climbing obstacles, a gun must be open and emptied of ammunition. These are a few basic guidelines when using shotguns in particular, though the principles still apply, whatever type of gun is in use.

What Gun to Use?

The .22 air rifle and the twelve-bore shotgun are the most popular for use when rabbit hunting, though the twenty-, or sixteen-bore is of lighter weight and is about as effective as the twelve-bore. A twelve-bore will be effective up to around

128

At ranges of more than forty yards you risk only wounding the rabbit, rather than cleanly killing it.

.22 air rifles are best suited to stalking rabbits.

forty yards, and number five or six shot is best used. The shotgun bore and shot size differ, and each has its own personal preference. My advice is to seek the assistance of your local gun dealer and then find out for yourself which best suits you. Remember that above forty yards there is a far greater chance of wounding, rather than killing, your quarry, so be choosy about the targets you shoot at, and always aim for the clean kill. And never increase your shot size, thinking that this will increase distances at which rabbits can be taken. Using shot that is intended for fox or geese will only tear your rabbit to pieces

and make it inedible, even to dogs and ferrets. A friend of mine was experimenting with shot size and chose one that was too heavy for rabbits. A rabbit was bolted by my ferret and came running towards him. He took aim and fired, blasting his quarry into little shreds. It was unrecognizable as a rabbit and his shot size was very quickly changed to something more suitable.

Rabbits can be controlled by shooting on the lamp too, but there are now stricter guidelines for night shooting, and it would be best to consult the BASC before you engage in this activity, because recent accidents have focused attention on night shooting from the safety aspect. My advice is to start with an air rifle for walked-up rabbits in daylight, and to use a twelve-bore shotgun for taking ferreted and bushed rabbits – air rifles and bullet guns are not at all suited to this type of shooting. In fact, bullet guns are best used for larger quarry such as deer and foxes and are not really suited to rabbit hunting, though some may disagree with this. I do not see the point of using bullet guns for rabbits, when a .22 air rifle can be used, together with fieldcraft, to take them.

The early morning and the evening are the best times for stalking rabbits, and camouflage clothing is best worn. This form of hunting is extremely exciting and is most effective and rewarding. Remember to stalk carefully and silently though, because feeding rabbits always have a sentry on duty, and each will take turns in scanning the horizon and nearby undergrowth for signs of imminent danger. Once you are spotted, a drummer will sound its warning and you will be left with an empty field. Bullet guns can be used for rabbits at long distances, and a friend of mine took many using this method; but the fieldcraft element is gone. Rabbits will remain out feeding even after they see danger, as long as it stays at a distance, so it is easy to shoot them in this way. However, the excitement of stalking with an air rifle and getting close enough to take the target is what gives this form of hunting its thrill.

To my mind, fieldcraft is by far the best method, and is as important as the shooting itself. Scopes will be necessary, even when stalking to close range, for this allows for a more accurate shot. Body shots are effective, but most rabbits will look about them for several seconds at a time, making head shots much more accessible – in fact they often make it easy for the sporting shooter. As long as those sights are accurately set (something that should be checked thoroughly before you start out), then taking rabbits in this way, as long as proper fieldcraft is exercised, is not at all difficult. Rabbits looking about them in this way offer a clear target to the shooter: they are a veritable sitting duck, just asking for it.

Shotguns are of no use whatsoever for stalking rabbits. When using an air rifle, the other rabbits, when one of their companions is shot, will often carry on feeding as though nothing has happened, meaning that quite a few can be taken during just one stalk. With shotguns, of course, the blast would send every other rabbit scurrying for cover, and you would only ever be able to take two, at the most, with each stalk. .22 air rifles are by far the best for this, as the .177 is just not powerful enough for effective rabbit shooting, and injuries, rather than clean kills, would be far more likely. However, when it comes to shooting ferreted and bushed rabbits, one can do no better than use a shotgun. A twelve- or a twenty-bore, if you prefer a lighter weight gun, are incredibly effective, but many have used .410 shotguns for this form of hunting, and with great success. The trouble is, this smaller gun is nowhere near as effective as the larger twelve-bore, and so woundings will occur far more often. Derek Webster engaged in rabbit shooting when he was younger with this type of gun and took many with it, as did Roy, a hunting friend of mine; but still, I would not recommend a shotgun of this size.

*The .410 used by
Derek Webster
during his poaching
days as a young lad.*

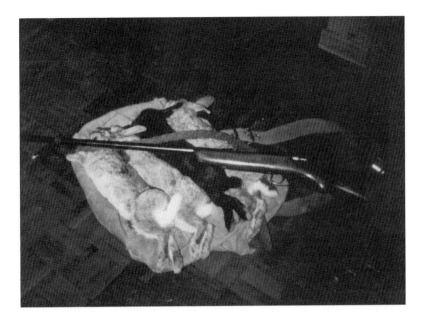

Make certain a ferret is not on the back of a rabbit before shooting, or releasing a hawk.

Sometimes I used purse nets.

Shooting Safely

Whether rabbits are ferreted or bushed using dogs, they bolt at incredible speed, and the shooter must have his wits about him, always being safety conscious and only firing when a clear shot is available.

- First, you should mark exactly where fellow hunters are stood, preferably behind the gun handler, and where the bushing dogs are.
- Also, sometimes ferrets can come out of a warren on the back of a running rabbit, so the shooter must make certain that no ferret is attached.
- If a rabbit stops in the mouth of the warren, then wait for it to run well clear before taking a shot, for a ferret may have hold of it.

- Likewise, do not take shots at rabbits that stop just outside undergrowth, for a dog could be just behind it and in the line of fire. Again, wait for a clear shot.
- If you feel your quarry is out of range and is at risk of being wounded, rather than cleanly killed, then allow it to run for another day.
- When using darker coloured dogs, never fire at a target you think, or presume, is the quarry. Make certain of your target before firing, lest a mistake occurs and a dog is accidentally killed.
- Common sense is vital, as important as proper licensing and having permission to shoot on the land you hunt.

When ferreting for guns, and falconers too, it is vital to use locators, because the last thing these people want is to spend their day waiting for a ferret to emerge. If a kill occurs, then speed is of the essence, and a quick recovery is only usually attained with the use of locators. Locators are becoming more advanced, and at the time of writing a new one is coming on the market: the ferret finder mark 2. I can see the day coming when a tiny microchip will be injected under the skin of the scruff of the neck and a small receiver box used to pinpoint, to within a millimetre, the ferret's location! Accurate marks are vital, for the digger could so easily kill or injure a fitch when breaking through to the tunnel, if he was not aware of how close he was. Locators are wonderful inventions and they are especially useful when shooting and hawking ferreted rabbits.

Doing the ferreting for guns is very exciting indeed, and much employment will be enjoyed by your fitches. When I first started with ferrets, I did a great deal of ferreting for two particular shooting men, Ian and Graham. They used twelve-bore shotguns, using number six shot as I remember, and we took large hauls of rabbits when we teamed up. Sometimes I would use purse nets and they would help despatch those caught, while at other times they were bolted and shot – though quite a few still got away using this method.

Shotgun safety was deeply impressed on my mind in those early days, after I witnessed a very close shave indeed. Ian and Graham had recently purchased two new guns, and we were trying them out for the first time on that late summer morning. We were out long before dawn and had to walk through town in order to get to our hunting grounds, just as dawn was breaking, where we did much poaching. The farmers obviously knew we were on their land (how could they not have done with those blasts ringing out regularly?), but they left us alone, no doubt content in the knowledge that we were reducing the rabbit population, for there were plenty about and damage to pasture was rife. I was ferreting rabbits along a riverbank and Ian and Graham stood close by, awaiting the bolting coneys. Ian loaded, and then Graham, but as he closed the barrel, the cartridge fired. We all nearly jumped out of our skin, but none more so than Graham, for the shot had just missed Ian's head. Graham was deathly pale and in some shock, for he realized just how close he had come to killing his friend and hunting partner.

That incident taught vital lessons. For one thing, never point a gun at anything but your intended target, and make certain that the gun is pointing where it can do no harm when loading. There was a fault with the firing pin on this gun, and Graham quickly got it mended, but we had come very close to disaster on that morning. Shotgun safety cannot be stressed enough!

Permission to Hunt

Having written permission is also just as vital. I did a lot of poaching in those days, even using illegally carried guns, but I would never dream of doing such things nowadays, and I strongly encourage all hunters to make sure they are fully licensed and have permission to shoot on land they visit. Again, the importance of these things cannot be stressed enough!

CHAPTER 9

RABBITING WITH HAWKS

Hawking is an ancient form of hunting, and has got to be one of the most exciting of all country pursuits. Kings would ride out on horseback and fly hawks, falcons and eagles at a variety of different quarry, but here we are mainly concerned with rabbits, and although this pursuit can still be carried out on horseback – and is in some countries – the rabbit-hunting man will be on foot, a bushing dog by his side, ferret in box and hawk on hand. As with shooting, a team of two or more is most effective, for one can do the ferreting, while others release the birds after the rabbits have bolted.

Hawks, falcons, eagles: all are temperamental, and it takes real skill to properly train such birds. By this I mean flying a bird that is responsive to its owner when flown at a decent weight, rather than a bird that needs to be half-starved before it will fly. Of course, the proper flying weight will vary between birds, and experimentation is the best way of measuring this; but if your bird cannot cope with a moderate wind, battling against it in vain and being blown every which way, then it is far too light. True, blustery days are not well suited to flying hawks, as they can be blown off course and are at greater risk of flying into dangerous obstacles, but still, they should be able to cope well enough with lighter winds.

Which Hawk to Choose?

Some birds are easier to train than others. The Harris hawk, for instance, is more

A peregrine falcon, more suited to grouse and pigeons.

easily trained and often more responsive than a goshawk or a peregrine falcon. One important advantage of flying Harris hawks is that they are not likely to sit sulking in trees for hours on end until they are hungry enough to fly back to the fist. Buzzards can be most irritating for this, and many have been lost when they have simply flown away. Melvyn Westwood flew a buzzard, and one day it simply flew from the fist and would not return. He heard many reports of a large bird flying around with jesses on, dangling from its legs as it flew overhead, but he never saw it again.

Harris hawks, being usually more responsive than other types of hawking bird, have recently become more popular, especially for the hunting of quarry such as rats and rabbits. For those interested only in quarry of this type, then the Harris hawk is an ideal purchase, ranging in price at the time of writing from around £100 to £300, the males being cheaper, as they are smaller and thus not quite as useful as a female.

One of the most exciting birds to fly has got to be the peregrine falcon, though they are mainly for taking grouse and pigeons, their natural prey. When I was out with Melvyn Westwood, he sent his peregrine on and it flew high into the air, suddenly plummeting at incredible speed and hitting a wood pigeon, before rising and circling again, coming in to claim its prize. That pigeon was hit so hard that feathers billowed from it on impact. It then fell to the ground rapidly, like a heavy stone, yet we could find not a single trace of it. There were two explanations for what had happened. Either a predator was in the area where the bird fell and it claimed the prize for itself, dragging it into cover where we could not detect it, or that bird had survived the attack and had crept away into the undergrowth. We were baffled, but none more so than Meg, Mel's falcon! Meg once attacked a magpie, chasing it all over the place as it attempted to shake off the falcon, among the wispy branches of a lonely tree at the foot of the moors. It would certainly have perished, had it not been for the fact that a pair of ravens began mobbing her, driving her away and unintentionally saving the life of that fortunate magpie.

Training the Hawk

A fat hawk will usually be unresponsive, so you must work at getting the weight just right. This will differ with each individual bird, but one thing remains constant with every hawk: the need to have them at the correct weight and in fine, fit condition. Falconers' birds must be in tiptop condition if they are to perform well in the field. This means regular flying sessions to the fist and the lure. Make training sessions a positive experience for the bird, rewarding it with titbits when appropriate and keeping the sessions fairly short.

They must become familiar with ferrets and bushing dogs, too. Have your ferret cage close to the aviary where they can easily be seen, and feed your bird close to the cage while the ferrets are active. The same thing can be done with dogs. When feeding your bird, allow your dog to accompany you to the aviary, though keep it outside. When walking the bird in the countryside, something that is essential if you are going to get your hawk familiar with its surroundings, with farm animals, other birds and even ramblers and cars, is to take your dog along and keep it by your side at first, allowing it to roam and hunt

Make sure your hawk has a good chance of catching its quarry.

around, once the bird is familiar with its presence. Once the hawk associates dogs and ferrets with pleasurable experiences, the battle is half won. It is now time to begin hunting with it.

Starting Hunting with a Hawk

The most effective way is to start with the dog straightaway. A greater number of rabbits will afford a greater opportunity for success, and a bushing dog is invaluable for this. The best type, in my opinion, is a spaniel. Terriers and lurchers are, of course, wonderful bushing dogs, but the lurcher will give chase just as keenly as the hawk, and the terrier will eagerly rush in for the kill while the bird is on its quarry. This could mean serious injury, even death, for the hawk, should the terrier grab the bird by mistake, not to men-

tion injury to the dog, as a striking hawk could easily take a terrier's eye out. Spaniels have great noses and will flush rabbits from even dense cover.

When an easier flight presents itself, release the bird and hopefully it will make a kill. The earlier the success, the more confident the bird will become, which is why it is essential only to fly the bird at rabbits you think will make an easier catch. A bird flown at every rabbit, when it is obvious the bird cannot possibly succeed, will only destroy confidence and make the whole experience distasteful, thus ensuring an unresponsive bird. Once a few kills have been made from the fist, then you can fly the bird from a tree, or a gate or fence post. This leaves you free to help with the ferreting. Once a bird can be left in this way, it makes it easier for those who hunt alone, carrying out the ferreting themselves.

When your bird makes a kill, it is important to make certain that the dog does not run in and grab the quarry. Encourage the dog to sit quietly while the bird eats some of the prize. Do not take the bird up straightaway (easier said than done), but allow it to be rewarded for its efforts – though do not allow the bird to gorge itself either, for then it may not be fit for flight again that day.

Once the hawk comes to associate the ferret with bolting rabbits, it will not be interested in attacking your fitch, which, after all, is an ally. After a few outings, the dog, hawk and ferret will be a formidable team, and quite large numbers of rabbits can be taken in this way.

If you don't wish to keep dogs and ferrets, then rabbiting with hawks alone is still an option, though the numbers of rabbit taken will be far less, and this form of hunting is in no way effective as a means of pest control. During the early morning or evening, when rabbits are out feeding, you can walk the fields and fly your bird at suitable targets – those bunnies that are feeding far away enough from home, or undergrowth. Fieldcraft can

be enjoyed in this way, but as I said, you will make far fewer kills. Stalking rabbits and then releasing the bird is a very exciting form of hunting, however, and some great flights will be witnessed. Do not forget that hawks, falcons and eagles fly at incredible speeds, and can be on top of their quarry in no time at all. This makes the success rate far higher, though misses will also be numerous.

Carl Noon of Nottingham normally hunts with Harris hawks, but he has recently purchased a Red-Tailed hawk, and this bird looks promising. He was standing in his yard, a small plot of land where he keeps his aviary and his ferrets, with this bird of prey and a rat was lurking around a small drainpipe. The hawk saw it and Carl let it go, and the bird killed a buck rat in fine style: so Carl has high hopes for future hunting with his Red-Tailed hawk. These have a reputation for being more difficult to train and for being less responsive than Harris hawks, but the truth is that it takes a great deal of skill and patience to train any bird of prey.

A buzzard. These can be useful rabbiting birds, but do not compare to Harris hawks.

Carl Noon with his American Red-Tailed Hawk.

One of the funniest things I ever saw was a hunt that Melvyn Westwood and Storm, his buzzard, took part in. Mel spotted a rabbit squatting on a hillside and he stalked it, moving swiftly but silently across the rough ground, with Storm on his fist and his dog close to heel. Scooby was the

Scanning the woodland floor from a good vantage point.

dog's name and Mel called him a lurcher, but he was a proper mongrel who looked very much like Scooby-doo, whom he was named after. He was the most stupid dog I have ever come across, and was forever bumping into things and banging his head. Mel was getting ever closer to his quarry and the buzzard scanned the ground, experience telling her that a rabbit was around somewhere. The stalk was exciting to watch and I felt that Mel was getting ready to release his bird when, suddenly, he disappeared from view into a ditch, with Storm fluttering wildly to get free. He let go, the rabbit ran and was quickly into its warren, and Scooby, instead of attempting to catch the quarry, thought some sort of daft game was going on and leapt through the air, landing on Mel's back, grabbing his flat cap and pulling it off his head, together with a large chunk of his hair, and then ran off with it. Mel, his temper getting the better of him, eventually scrambled to his feet and chased after his dog who easily kept out of his way, dodging this way and that and growling menacingly, but in jest, at his owner who was livid, not yet having seen the funny side.

Pinning its prey to the ground.

With patience and perseverance, a bird of prey can be taught to become part of an efficient rabbiting team consisting of man, dog, ferret and hawk. It may take a few outings, but eventually the hawk will come to regard all in the partnership as allies, and so will quickly know the part it must play. A few basic guidelines must be observed, such as providing dry and draught-free sleeping quarters; plenty of good food, for a bird must not be kept on the verge of starvation in order to make it more obedient – though of course, hunger does play an important part in the training process; and being safety conscious while out in the field. One thing to be careful of, as is the case when shooting, is to make certain that a ferret is not on the back of a bolting rabbit when a bird is loosed.

I was out recently with Derek Webster and Chris Dewhurst, high in the Yorkshire Dales where Derek clears rabbits, which do much damage to pasture and young trees. A group of falconers were across the other side of the dale and we watched as the spaniels flushed coney from reeds and other undergrowth. Hawks were then loosed, some from the fist, others from the top of walls or from rocky outcrops. We naturally got on to the subject of falconry and of how it can be a frustrating game, for the weather must be right, and the weight and condition of the bird must also be near-perfect. 'Aye,' said Chris, looking at Derek, his hunting partner, 'Derek's a bit like that, yuh know, he 'as to be at the reyt weight an' all. He 'as to be at least eighteen stone before he can come ferretin'!'

APPENDIX I

Suppliers of Rabbiting Equipment

Ian Hodge Shooting & Fieldsports
   Supplies
Wadebridge
Cornwall PL27 7LA
Tel. 01208 813652

Target Sports of Bolton
486 Halliwell Road
Bolton
Lancs BL1 8AN
Tel. 0870 0607331

Johnson Field Sports
Ireland Close
Staveley
Chesterfield, S43 3PE
Tel. 0800 73 11 798

Arthur Carter Field Sports
Unit 4
Cavans Way
Binley Industrial Estate
Coventry CV3 2SF
Tel. 02476 454 244

Attleborough Accessories Dept
C.W. Morley
St Peter
Norfolk NR18 9TZ
Tel. 01953 454932

KP&S Nets
Hunter's Cross
Yawl Hill Lane
Uplyme
Dorset DT7 3RW
Tel. 01297 33920 or 07768 222348

Brinded Nets
Fairview
Mybster
Watten
Wick
Caithness KW1 5XW.
Tel. 07879 690694 or 07984 971040
(only mobile numbers available at time of writing)

APPENDIX II

Tips on Keeping Hunting Permission

- Make certain that dogs are fully broken to all farm livestock, including cats.
- Always backfill and make the area neat and tidy after digging out ferret and rabbit.
- Respect livestock and property, mending fences and so on, which may be broken while climbing over.
- Never leave a ferret. If you cannot afford a locator, then make certain you are willing to wait for the return of your fitch when it makes a kill below. Purchase a locator as soon as you can afford one.
- Be willing to spend a little time chatting to the landowner, or helping out if needed.
- Take all litter home and put it in your own bin.
- If a farmer requests that a warren be cleared and filled in, comply with his wishes.

INDEX